PIANO

Gillian Shepheard

TEACH YOURSELF BOOKS

For UK orders: please contact Bookpoint Ltd,
130 Milton Park, Abingdon, Oxon OX14 4SB.
Telephone: (44) 01235 827720, Fax: (44) 01235 400454.
Lines are open from 9.00-18.00, Monday to Saturday,
with a 24-hour message answering service.
Email address: orders@bookpoint.co.uk

For U.S.A. order enquiries: please contact
McGraw-Hill Customer Services, P.O. Box 545, Blacklick,
OH 43004-0545, U.S.A.
Telephone: 1-800-722-4726. Fax: 1-614-755-5645.

For Canada order enquiries: please contact
McGraw-Hill Ryerson Ltd., 300 Water St, Whitby,
Ontario L1N 9B6, Canada.
Telephone: 905 430 5000. Fax: 905 430 5020.

Long renowned as the authoritative source for self-guided learning –
with more than 30 million copies sold worldwide – the *Teach Yourself*
series includes over 300 titles in the fields of languages, crafts,
hobbies, business and education.

British Library Cataloguing in Publication Data
A catalogue record for this title is available from The British Library

Library of Congress Catalog Card Number: On file

First published in UK 2002 by Hodder Headline Plc.,
338 Euston Road, London NW1 3BH

First published in US 2002 by Contemporary Books,
A Division of The McGraw-Hill Companies,
1 Prudential Plaza, 130 East Randolph Street, Chicago,
Illinois 60601 U.S.A.

The 'Teach Yourself' name and logo are rgistered trade marks of
Hodder & Stoughton Ltd.

Cover photo from Photodisc
Typeset by Dorchester Typesetting Group Ltd.
Printed in Great Britain for Hodder & Stoughton Educational,
a division of Hodder Headline Plc, 338 Euston Road,
London NW1 3BH by J. W. Arrowsmith Ltd., Bristol.

Impression number 10 9 8 7 6 5 4 3 2 1
Year   2007 2006 2005 2004 2003 2002

Contents

Dedication

This book is dedicated to my very first and dearest piano teacher, Joan Bourlet, who showed me how to make lovely music from the black and white blobs, and to my superb professor, the late Sidney Harrison.

Also my own dear family for their continuous support and encouragement.

Huge thanks to Jo Armitage for her invaluable help in checking the ms with honesty and humour and the same to Slough Writers' Group for their enthusiastic support and constructive criticisms.

Thanks go to Brian Rhodes-Smith of Sheargold Pianos Ltd, Maidenhead, for readily answering my queries and helping me choose music to go with this book.

And, of course, to all my pupils over the years who have taught *me* how to pass my love of music on to *them*.

About the author

Gillian Shepheard studied piano full-time at the Guildhall School of Music and Drama in London. She has taught piano to students from ages 5 to 85 whose abilities ranged from prodigious to quite severely handicapped. Most past students continue to love their music, often using it for the benefit of their community.

Introduction: What is music?

Letters, words and punctuation are all ingredients of speech – but they are only ingredients. Whatever words we use and however strongly we feel, speaking in a flat monotone will not convey our pleasure, interest or fury.

It is exactly the same with music. Clefs, staves, notes and all the other musical signs are essential for conveying a composer's *ideas* but again they are only the ingredients of music. However much you feel the shapes and sounds 'inside you' if you play the keys in a solid, 'stompy' way you will project nothing of the musical meaning.

By following the suggestions in this book you will discover how to use your body to play the piano like a musician – brain, eyes and ears sending out instructions to your fingers, hands, arms – and even your feet! You will learn how to weigh and blend and coax the sounds you want from the piano keys – and how to listen to check that they are as near perfect as you can make them. Even if you can spare only a few minutes a day, with good, regular practice this will quickly become automatic. How soon you can begin to produce the sounds you want depends on careful listening and, to a certain extent, on your own natural ability.

One day you will suddenly find you are gaining far more from your playing than the initial satisfaction of 'getting the right keys down at the right time'. This is a really exciting moment! As soon as you can play even the simplest piece through without stopping, try to give it as much meaning as you can. Initially you can exaggerate the emotion – it is far easier to modify down than to build up. Judge your playing by metaphorically 'putting your ears on a nearby table' – and *listening*. Your interpretation will vary every time you play your piece. That is perfectly normal, for in any live art – music, dancing, acting, gymnastics, skating – there are differences in every performance, sometimes bringing a wonderful new light to the work; sometimes bringing it crashing down! Hopefully, you will soon fall in love with your piano and together you will produce the music as the composer intended.

In Shakespeare's *Twelfth Night*, Duke Orsino says: 'If music be the food of love, play on . . . '

I say: 'Love your music – and now get started!'

Get set up

I would imagine that you have often wished you could play the piano. Perhaps you had a few lessons as a child but you wouldn't practise or you didn't get on with your teacher.

As with any new long-term interest, there are times when taking up the piano is impractical. Such as the first two years after the birth of your twins. Or a month before you are transferred overseas. Otherwise life's normal awkwardness needs present no real obstacle to teaching yourself to play well enough to get tremendous satisfaction and pleasure from making your own music and even entertaining your friends.

Your two most important requirements are to put by a regular 15–30 minutes every day for practice and the determination to keep going even when you feel you aren't getting on as quickly as you'd hoped. At these times look back. You couldn't have done this, or you didn't know that, a month ago!

Try to maintain the 'everyday' routine, since continually attempting to catch up with an extra hour on Sunday just doesn't work, any more than an athlete could win a marathon if he only trained once a week.

There are really no shortcuts to learning to play the piano – but there are far more interesting ways than the old-fashioned tedium of hours of scales and complicated theory.

You can make a start even if you haven't yet obtained your piano. Find a table of keyboard height – between 2′4″ and 2′6″ (approximately 74–76 cms) – and a comfortable seat. The latter must be high enough for you to sit with your forearms level with the tabletop.

On this simulated 'table-piano' practise 1, 2 and 3 (as in Unit 2) for five to ten minutes every day and you will be beginning to grasp the basics of good piano playing and establishing your regular practice routine by the time your piano arrives.

Start training yourself to 'listen'. Listening will help you to discover how to make the sounds you want. Playing the right notes is important but playing them in the right way is much more so. So wake up your ears by consciously listening to the birds; to the sounds of the day; of the night. And borrow a few CDs of piano music from your library.

Look ahead. Just as an artist varies his use of paints to capture a bleak or sunny scene, so will you aim to play each piece like a music-picture, conveying the mood and colour. Once your brain/ear/finger coordination is automatic – which, with practice, will gradually happen – you will have grasped the two essential aspects of piano playing: how to vary your touch to get the sounds you want and how to check by listening.

Just because you really want to play don't expect to be able to perform your favourite Gershwin in a few weeks. If that were possible everyone would be doing it but if you stick to your daily piano time through dreary chore or demanding chairman you will be amazed at your progress.

Once you can understand how written music 'works' you will be able to explore any pieces you want that are within your current playing ability. And after a few days with your piano and Unit 3, musical notation will not be a problem.

Whether you later want to play to, or with, other people is entirely up to you. Trying out simple duets with other pianists (duets are often arranged for beginner and advanced pianist) or with an instrumentalist such as a flautist or a violinist, can be highly rewarding, exciting and inspiring and drive you on to learn new pieces.

Solo performing to family and friends of even your earliest pieces is a different challenge altogether from playing with other musicians. While a few of us excel in front of an audience, most do not play quite as well in public as when alone.

This does not apply only to adults. At competitive music festivals some of the keenest and most musical youngsters will play overcautiously, losing the flow and sparkle of the music, while others – who may be neither as musical nor as hard working – adopt a 'devil may care' confidence and carry off the medals.

It isn't fair. But it happens. There are ways of overcoming stage fright but those are for a later chapter.

Most local libraries have music sections containing collections by composers whose names you may have heard but whose compositions you believe to be far out of your reach. Yet many of the great composers wrote simple but amazingly beautiful music for their own student beginners – and those you, too, will soon be able to play and love.

But to basics.

Your first essential, of course, is a piano.

Pianos vary wildly in quality, size and price. From new, full-sized concert grands to second-hand uprights there are pianos to suit every budget and every home. Like cars, the range and value for money is almost limitless.

However beautiful it looks in the showroom – and even if you could afford it – a full-sized concert grand piano is not a good buy if the only place it will fit is the garage. A baby grand or a fine upright is more practical for the average home. These have wide dynamic and tonal ranges. Avoid the neat little upright that would wedge perfectly under the stairs. Very small pianos have short strings and cannot produce the good full sounds of normal-sized uprights which are 'overstrung' – that is, to give them extra length and richer tone the bass strings are crossed diagonally behind the shorter treble strings – beneath them in a grand piano.

Never give houseroom to a really old and dilapidated instrument. Pianos have hundreds of working parts and eventually wear out in the same way cars do and come to the end of their useful lives.

Even experienced pianists get no pleasure or satisfaction from playing on a piano whose strings are rusty or whose felts are worn down or eaten away by moths.

Electronic keyboards with their range of fun buttons and backing sounds can be tempting but you are unlikely to get far with your own playing when pressing a button does it all for you. After a while you will become thoroughly bored, lacking the satisfaction of making the music for yourself. Further, some people complain of 'humming' in their ears after playing on one of these for any length of time. Even if the keys are touch sensitive (i.e. responding to the player's touch to produce loud or soft sounds) it cannot really be compared with that of a good acoustic, or normal, piano.

However, they are often less expensive to buy and, being usually more compact, do not take up too much space in a small room. Another advantage is that they never have to be tuned – unlike acoustic pianos that need a visit from the tuner two or three times a year. Earphones are a useful 'extra' when practising could disturb the neighbours.

If you already possess an electronic keyboard you can certainly make good progress on it to begin with so don't feel you must rush out at once to buy an acoustic piano.

Never consider buying one of the 'keyboards' that children crave for birthday presents. They are laptop in size and have minimal range – only three to four octaves instead of the seven plus of a normal piano and are not intended for pianists.

Decide where you are going to put your piano and measure the space. If you can arrange to have a window to one side so that the light can fall on the music so much the better. If natural light is impossible a bright standard lamp is next best.

You may be able to borrow a piano. Spread the word! Someone may be moving to a smaller house or it was originally bought for the kids to play – only they never do. You will probably have to pay the removal men but it's well worth that outlay for a good piano but politely decline the offer if the instrument sounds really awful even before it is moved.

Another place to find a piano is in the small ads.

Just as you would call upon a qualified mechanic to vet a second-hand car you are thinking of buying you will need to arrange for a piano tuner/technician to accompany you. Your local music shop will be able to recommend one. The small charge for spotting major defects, such as worn out felts, rusty strings or broken hammers can save you the considerably large sum of money it could cost to have your instrument reconditioned, thus making your 'bargain' very expensive indeed.

You could visit your local auction room. Once again, take the tuner/technician along on the viewing day. If this or that piano is picked out as a good buy at the estimated value measure it, match the size with where you want to put it in your home and decide whether to try for it. Don't be put off by its colour. You can always cover it or even paint it to suit your decor. It will probably sound tinny in the auction room but your technician will examine it to see if there are major problems or if it only needs tuning. If the latter, once settled in your home its sound can be transformed.

A music shop is probably the best source of pianos. These will be generally more expensive but if you can afford it, well worth the extra and could save you many weeks of discouraging search.

Besides new instruments that will give years of pleasure, most music shops sell reconditioned pianos. These are considerably cheaper than the new ones but a good original will still be a fine instrument. You may be able to hire and the hire costs deducted from the price if you later decide to buy it, although hire pianos are not usually of very good quality.

Discuss it with the manager, insist that you want an instrument with a pleasant tone and neither a heavy nor too light a touch. The manager will probably be able to play for you. If not, take along a friend who can try out several before you decide.

Be realistic. How much space can you spare? What are you prepared to pay?

Get the best piano you can afford.

You will also need a chair or stool. You may think that a purpose-made, adjustable – and expensive – piano stool is essential but this is not so. Any chair or stool of the right height, without arms and with a comfortable but firm seat is perfectly adequate.

What are you waiting for? Wake up your ears by making a list of everything you can hear and then start getting your fingers moving by 'practising' on that table!

Laying your foundations

Sitting in front of your new piano for the first time is hugely exciting – but where do you go from here? How do you start?

I still chuckle over a cartoon I once saw of two builders walking away from a newly constructed tower in Pisa. One was saying to the other: 'So what if we skimped a bit on the foundations? No one will ever know!' (source unknown)

Unlike those builders, you must lay good foundations! Give yourself a few days of 15–20 minutes a day to get the basics secure and you will be away. Keep a notebook to record your practice routine for each stage; jot down what you are finding difficult that needs a little extra time; after a few days look back and congratulate yourself for the skills you have already acquired. Plan to practise at a time when you are fresh. Those terrible twins, Coordination and Concentration, are essential companions for playing the piano but they do tend to go on strike at the end of a busy day.

1 The first essential is to sit comfortably. Before driving a strange car you would adjust your seat, perhaps add a back support and get the feel of the controls.

So it is with the piano. You will never get the sounds you want if your seat is too low or too high, too close to or too far away from the keyboard. Furthermore, if you are sitting badly you will quickly begin to suffer back, shoulder and probably neckache.

Your chair or stool should be firm but comfortable, reasonably wide and at a height that enables your forearms to be level with the keyboard when you sit correctly (see Figure 2.1).

2 Being careful not to hunch your shoulders, imagine they are the top of a crane supporting your arms – those long, swinging sections that position the clutching scoop – your wrists, hands and fingers. Swing your arms up and down and from side to side keeping the 'crane' image in mind.

Now rest your hands in your lap, then, with your wrists drooping, arc them high over the keys before lowering them gently onto the keyboard in a loose fist. Ease your arms up and down, in and out, feeling the freedom in your wrists. Then reverse the movement, lifting off the keyboard and back onto your lap.

ouch!

ouch!

■ Figure 2.1

If any part of you is tense your playing will suffer. Could an athlete run with stiff knees? Or an actor speak his lines with a rigid jaw?

Now do it the *wrong* way. Sitting at the keyboard lift your hands directly up from your lap to the keyboard. Can you feel the tension up the back of your hands, your arms and your shoulders? That tension will inhibit your playing; your arms will ache and the sounds will be stilted.

Concert pianists always make a 'lift on – lift off' movement before they begin to play. It may look like showing off (well, sometimes it *is* a little exaggerated!) but the aim is to get their arms lightly balanced so that their fingers can move freely from top to bottom of the keyboard, wherever the music takes them.

Every day warm up with 'lift on–lift off' half a dozen times until it becomes automatic whenever you sit at the keyboard. This may seem tedious when you are dying to get playing but everyone engaged in a physical activity has to warm up. Athletes, singers, show jumpers.
And pianists.

3 For playing the piano your fingers are numbered 1–5, the thumb being number 1 (see Figure 2.2).

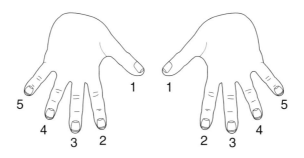

■ Figure 2.2

Shape your hands as if you are drumming your fingers impatiently on a tabletop. Do it on the lid of the keyboard. Is it as easy if your fingers are pencil straight or drooping like cooked spaghetti? It's amazing how many beginners try to play like that!

The position you need for playing is shown in Figure 2.3. Keep your hands 'soft', as if you are holding something fragile.

■ Figure 2.3

Ensuring your wrists 'give' and your arms are lightly supported by your shoulders, try this for finger independence:

'Lift on' as before. Rest the fingertips of one hand lightly on the keys and play any finger, depressing the key to sound without moving – without even twitching – any of the others. Rest – and repeat. Then try with another finger. (Your fourth finger is not totally independent and will not work as freely as the others.) After a few minutes repeat with the other hand.

In a day or so you can try with both hands together – watch carefully to ensure that the only fingers to move are those you want. Develop this little exercise over the next few weeks (while you are widening your musical experience) until you can play both hands together, two or three notes each and then with one hand ***staccato*** (quickly released, short sounds) and the other ***legato*** (smooth, joined sounds).

When you can do that try without watching your hands. Close your eyes, say aloud which fingers you are going to use, play them – then look to see if you were right. You will be amazed by how often you get this wrong! Brain/finger coordination!

This vital little exercise develops finger control and independence that will later make reading and playing music much easier. However, it does take solid concentration and five minutes are quite enough to spend on it in any one practice.

Look inside your piano. You will see wires, or strings, stretching downwards from the top of an upright piano – horizontally away from the keys in a grand piano.

One thick, coiled string for each deep bass key. (Play the extreme left keys and listen to the sounds.) Moving to the right each string splits into a pair of thinner ones, still coiled, for the next range as you climb up the keyboard. Finally the strings become as thin wires and are grouped three to each key.

While the long strings produce the lowest sounds, as they rise up to the highest sounds the strings become shorter until those at the extreme right of the piano are only a few inches long.

Resting on every string, or group of strings, is a little felt-lined block called a **damper**. This prevents the strings vibrating unless we play a key, causing the **hammer** to strike them (see Figure 2.4).

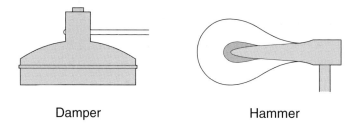

Damper   Hammer

■ Figure 2.4

At that instant the damper leaves the strings, allowing them to vibrate until we decide to release the key. You know the song: 'The head bone's connected to the neck bone . . . '? The keys, hammers and dampers are similarly connected.

Prove it for yourself. Play any key and watch the hammer strike the strings as the damper leaves them. While you hold the key down the strings are free to vibrate. It is this vibration that makes the sound. (Twanging an elastic band gives a similar, if limited result. Use a thick one for a low sound; a taut, thinner one for a high sound.)

Should the hammer remain touching the strings, or the damper fail to leave them, there would be no sound other than a soft dull thud. Experiment by using your finger as a damper and pressing it on the relevant strings while playing their key.

It follows that, to allow a sound to continue singing, the hammer immediately bounces back after striking the strings but the damper does not return to its normal position until you release the key. You can therefore control the duration of the sound by holding down its key as long as you want.

To make a loud sound you play a key down quickly. And for a soft sound play it slowly. Try it! Never press down into the key once the sound has been made for you cannot alter it. If you look inside the piano again you will see that once the hammer has struck the strings no amount of key pressing will make any difference. The making of the sound is finished! When you begin to play from printed music the type of note will show you how long each sound should last although all sounds eventually fade away naturally even when the keys are held down.

Now look again at the strings. Can you tell which belongs to which key? A wild guess may be right but inside the piano, within their groups of one, two and three, all strings look the same.

Many people initially eye the black keys with apprehension but seen simply as extensions of the hammers – as are all the white keys too – they become friendly aids to finding your way round the keyboard. Try standing a piece of paper in front of the black keys and you will realize how difficult it is to find the one you want. This will be clarified in the next unit.

🄳🄸🅂🄲 Time to experiment! Using the whole keyboard make up sounds to resemble: a snow scene; a thunderstorm; the tide coming in; two on a trampoline; rippling water. Use your body weight, arms, hands and any fingers as and how you like. Listen – and adjust your touch if necessary. This will help you to judge how to make the sounds you want without having to worry about playing specific notes.

Finally, close your eyes and try to play a soft sound with one hand at the same time as you play a loud one with the other. Were you conscious that for the quiet sound you played the key down slowly and quickly for the loud sound? Or did they both sound the same?

Don't worry. Getting one hand to sing a melody while the other hand plays a quiet accompaniment is a trick for later!

3

Getting your bearings

Spend the next 8–10 minutes of piano time on this but do not expect to grasp it all in one sitting. Once you have, you will quickly and easily be able to find any printed note, anywhere on the keyboard.

To understand the 'height' or 'depth' of sounds, the pitch, play the key on the extreme left of the keyboard. This makes a very low-pitched sound. Now play the key on the other end of the keyboard. That is a very high-pitched sound and, of course, there are many degrees of pitch in between.

Relating notes on the sheet music to their positions on the keyboard has traditionally been taught with mnemonics. If you had piano lessons as a child you were probably taught phrases like 'All Cows Eat Grass' and 'Every Good Boy Deserves Fun' as have been chanted by bored pupils – and their equally weary teachers! – ever since music lessons began. But these mnemonics were never relevant to music and while very keen students mastered notation – usually in their own ways – the majority more or less muddled through eventually.

There is an easy and logical three-stage way to understand the relationship between printed notes and their positions on the keyboard.

You will need a sheet of lined A4 paper, firmly backed and placed upright on the music rest, a pencil and a highlighter.

Stage 1: The musical alphabet consists of only seven letters, A–G inclusive. Ignoring the black keys for now, play the white key on the extreme left of the keyboard. On every normal-sized piano this is an 'A'. Write that letter *below* the lowest line on the paper.

The next key up is 'B'. Write '*B*' on the first line up.

The next key is 'C' – write that in the space immediately above the 'B' line.

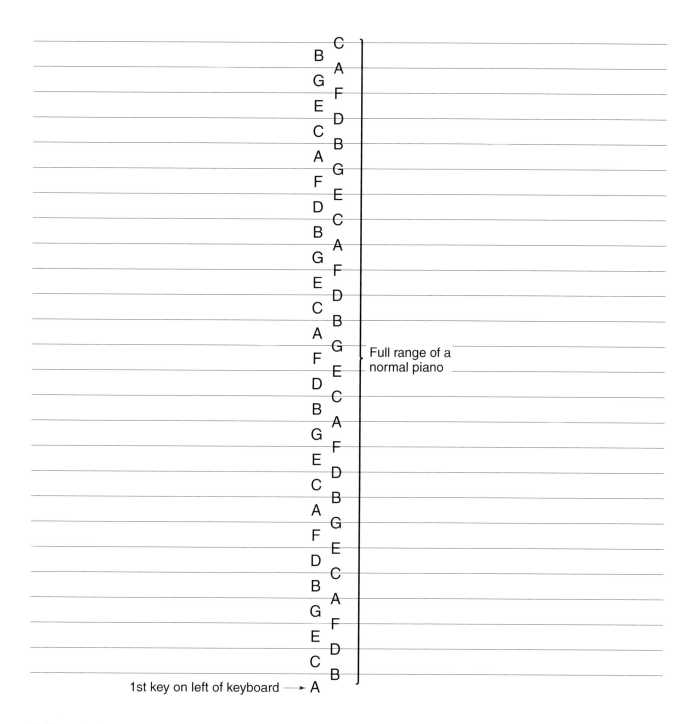

■ Figure 3.1 Stage 1

Continue thus up the alphabet to 'G', writing the letter-names on alternate lines and in the spaces between. Then start again with 'A'. You will see that this time the 'A' is on a line on your paper – it will be on alternate lines and spaces all the way up.

While the lowest key of a piano keyboard is always 'A' the highest can vary by a key or two. Do not worry about this. You will rarely, if ever, need to use these keys.

A normal-sized piano keyboard has eight 'A's and probably also an eighth 'B' and a 'C' to complete.

The distance between each 'A' (as between every other letter-name) is called an 'octave'. Eight keys apart and a comfortable stretch for most adult hands.

If you play two or more keys with the same letter-name you will find that they sound the same, varying only in 'pitch'.

See Figure 3.1. Stage 1.

Stage 2: Look at the whole keyboard, then at your paper and think for a moment.

Supposing you are about to try to learn a piece, wouldn't it take a long time to work out where the notes were? So many lines and spaces to count up!

Music was originally sung, the piano being a comparatively modern instrument (only about 500 years old). The lowest keys, therefore – and the highest ones – are useful for huge chords or for attempting to reproduce feelings of limitless ecstasy but they are not needed most of the time.

So, where are the songs? Male and female voices range over the middle of the keyboard and that is where most of our melodies are written.

Count up to the second G on the keyboard and highlight its line on your paper. Find it again on the keyboard. When you see a note on that line that is the key you will play!

This is where it helps to look at the cluster of three black keys to fix its position. From there you can quickly find all the other Gs using the black key clusters as a guide.

You will gradually come to associate the other named keys with their position in the two or three black key clusters without needing to know their letter-names.

In fact, **the second G on the keyboard is the only name you need to remember**. You will find all the other notes by **interval** – the distance between any two successive notes.

Attempting to recall the names of all the notes before playing them would make for a very slow and jerky performance. We simply judge the intervals between each, much as you gauge your footsteps up a flight of uneven treads. Everyone trips up sometimes! But, until you are familiar with the feel of the distances between the keys, find your place by counting up from the second G.

Return to your paper. It is time to clarify your position.

On your A4 page you have highlighted the second G line. Now highlight along the next four lines up.

This covers the piano keys through the lines and in the intervening spaces from the second G to nine keys above – A.

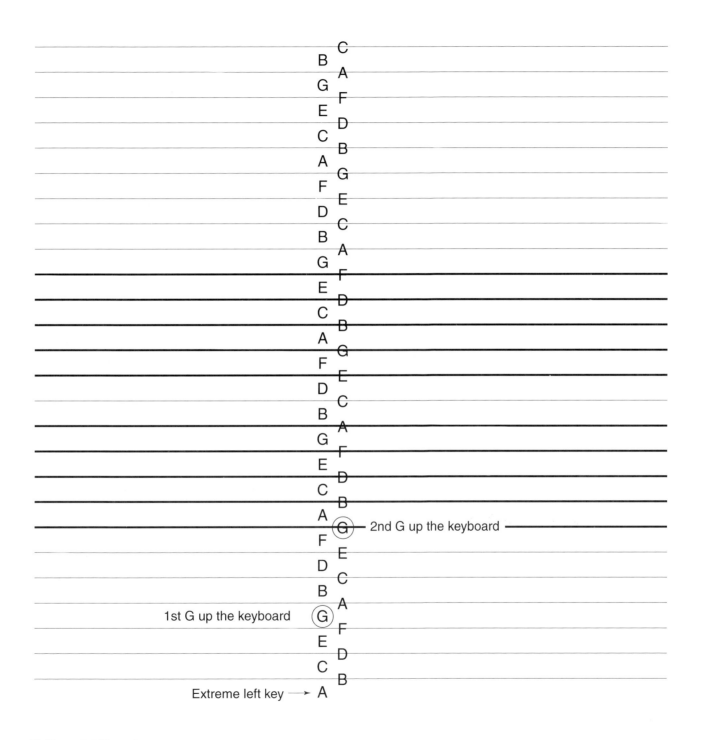

Figure 3.2 Stage 2

You now have five highlighted lines, one for each finger of your left hand. Play them up and down, using fingers 5–4–3–2–1. Listen to the sounds. Notice how they skip the keys in the spaces. Play the spaces too.

Miss out the next line up. This is known as middle C and, in keyboard music, its line is never drawn in its entirety.

Highlight the following five lines up. If you check with your written letter-names you will find these ascend from E to F. You now have a line for each finger of your right hand. Play them up and down using fingers 1–2–3–4–5, again listening to the sounds. Play the spaces.

Feel free to sing as many as you like from either **stave**.

See Figure 3.2 for completed Stage 2.

Stage 3: On your paper you can see that by highlighting the lines you have started to position the notes – but you could still group any five lines together and they would look the same as any other five!

Composers show us precisely *where* to play by placing signs, called **clefs**, at the start of each set of five lines. There are five clefs altogether, each to cover the range for individual instruments such as the viola or the bassoon but the piano uses only two, the treble clef and the bass clef.

Take the lower set and draw the sign shown in Figure 3.3.

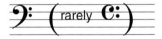

■ Figure 3.3

This is called the bass clef (sometimes the F clef as it begins on the F line) and it roughly covers the range of the male voice. It shows exactly on which part of the keyboard you will be playing. This set of highlighted lines is known as the bass stave and we usually play notes written there with our left hand.

Now move up to your other set of five highlighted lines and draw the sign shown in Figure 3.4.

■ Figure 3.4

This sign is called the treble clef (sometimes the G clef as it begins on a G line). This, too, shows exactly which keys are to be played. Your five highlighted lines within this compass make up the treble stave and the notes on it are usually played with the right hand.

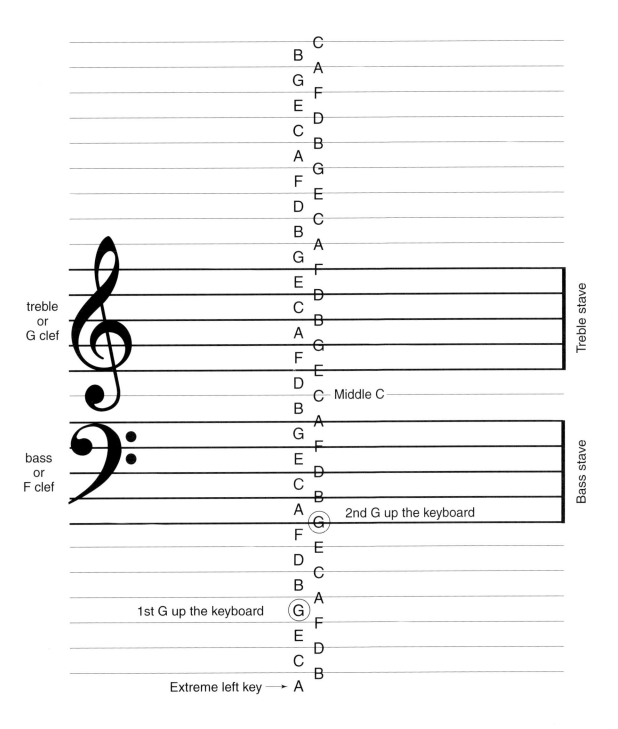

Figure 3.5 Stage 3

The treble and bass staves are always 'pulled apart' by a few extra millimetres, giving us two distinct groups of five lines. When middle C is to be played short sections of its line are placed near either the bass or treble stave according to which hand is to play the note.

Unless middle C is to be played there is no sign to mark its presence.

Your page now looks like this – and is complete.

See Figure 3.5 for completed Stage 3.

If a piece, or part of a piece, is written so that one hand cannot comfortably play the notes on its stave, the other hand can 'help out'. In duets, where four hands play, one person will probably play with both hands in the bass stave and the other person with both hands in the treble stave.

You can now see the whole keyboard on your paper but as we rarely use the very high or very low keys it is unnecessary to print the whole keyboard out (as shown in Figure 3.5) on every page of music.

Apart from wasting a great deal of paper it would make a book very expensive, far too thick to fit on any music rest – and almost too heavy to carry! Hence only the highlighted section, the treble and bass staves, are repeated over and over again down each page.

All the other lines and spaces are still there, as are the outer keys on the keyboard, ready and eager for you to compose that soaring spinning firework or cascading, silvery waterfall.

When we do need to play these outer notes small portions of the relevant lines are drawn parallel to the stave lines (as in Figure 3.1), as many above or below as needed to reach the printed note, showing where it can be found on the keyboard.

These added bits of lines are, like the middle C line, called leger lines.

Now look back. In just a few days you have learned the basics of fine piano playing. How to sit. How to find your way round the keyboard. Most importantly, how to start to produce the sounds you want.

Apportion your piano time to allow for every section you are currently working on. If you spend the whole time on, say, getting your fingers to work independently, your pieces will fall back. Keep everything up, every day, even if you cannot always fit in your full time at the piano.

List the sections in your notebook, adding to them or cutting out those you have finished with as you progress. Start off now with:

1 Sit comfortably. Lift on – lift off. Check hands shape. Finger exercise.

2 Play any key on the keyboard and find its position on your paper. Then reverse the process. In a few days this should speed up. More so if you can get someone else to call them out for you.

3 Sounds. As well as those I have suggested (thunder, seascape etc.), make up some of your own. It may seem childishly simple but why give yourself complicated notes to learn when the essential technique of adjusting your touch to suit the sounds you are trying to make is the whole point of this exercise?

Well done! You have grasped the essential fact that, while playing the right notes is important, playing them the right way to convey the mood is far more so.

4

Your first piece

Recite this verse aloud a couple of times, emphasizing the difference between strong and weak syllables:

Other people seem to set

Their lives upon an even keel

So why is it I always get

The trolley with the wonky wheel?

Now look through this short piece of music that goes with those words (Figure 4.1).

Where, with the whole keyboard before you, should this piece be played?

We have treble and bass staves, bracketed together to show that one person is to play all notes on either stave, but here the bass stave is blank, the tune being only on the treble stave and for the right hand. The second line is simply a continuation of the first.

Look again along the lines of notes. (Even experienced musicians look through a new piece of music before plunging in!) Almost throughout, the melody moves step by step (in 'seconds') up or down. There are a few places where the notes skip a space or a line (up or down a 'third') and towards the end there is one place where it skips a space and a line – two notes, which, counting both played notes (lowest to highest) we call a fourth.

Overall, the melody has a sort of switchback shape.

NB Where a note is skipped, rest its finger on its key, using the next finger for the following note of the melody.

Using Unit 3 Figure 3.5 as a guide, count up from your second G on the keyboard to find the first note. You will soon be able to link printed notes to piano keys without working them out but for now it is safer to count up. Our brains love getting fresh information – but hate correcting mistakes so always

piano

The Pessimist

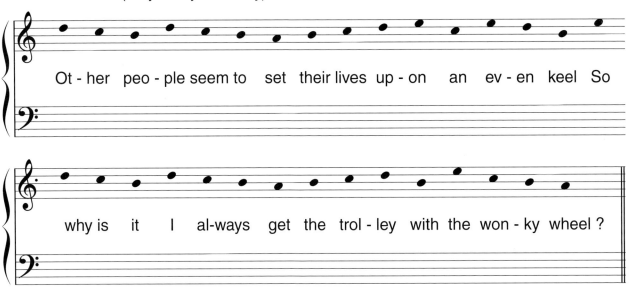

Andante dolente (fairly slowly and sadly)

Ot - her peo - ple seem to set their lives up - on an ev - en keel So

why is it I al-ways get the trol - ley with the won - ky wheel ?

■ Figure 4.1

aim to play the right notes every time.

Lift your right hand onto the keys and lay your curved fingers lightly over them. Check through the piece again. If you place your fifth finger over the highest key – the 11th note through the piece – you will start with your fourth finger and will have enough fingers to cover every key used in the melody.

As a double check, using the Chapter 3 reference, you will see the highest note is E and the lowest is A. The melody begins with the fourth finger on D.

You are now ready to play through the piece carefully. Play it twice more, familiarizing yourself with the melody and, listening acutely, slightly stressing the strong notes that go with the strong syllables as you would naturally do in speech.

Now play it a little faster – let the music move in a nice curve, now with only the lightest emphases, as you would if you were singing the words. It is obviously not a fast piece but it does need to flow along easily.

As it stands it can be quite difficult to follow. It is like written prose without punctuation. Take a pencil. In music the stronger stresses, or **beats**, are shown by drawing a vertical line from top to bottom of the staves immediately before each. These are called bar lines and the distance between each is called a bar.

In a piece without words it could be difficult to know where the stresses should be but a bar line shows that *the beat immediately following it is the stressed one*. (There is no need to draw a bar line at the beginning of the piece as there is one just before the clef.) You may feel that this piece has alternate strong–weak syllables (duple time) but emphasizing alternate beats (and words) would make it sound stilted.

Quadruple time, with a stress every fourth beat, suits it better so draw your first bar line just before the fifth note (the word 'seem'), then the ninth note ('lives'), to give four syllables, and notes, to each bar.

Continue through the piece to the last bar, then finish it off with ‖ (double bar lines):

O-ther peo-ple | SEEM to set their | LIVES up-on an | E-ven keel etc.

When you play, there is no need to 'thump' out the main beats any more than you would exaggerate strong syllables in speech. Feeling always towards the next bar and leaning slightly into its first note is all that is needed for the music to make sense.

Now draw a 'tail' (sometimes called 'stem') on each note. Tails are shortish, straight lines down or up from the side of each note. This gives each one beat, or 'count', to match the syllables. Keep these 'tails' as much within the stave as possible i.e. the first five notes have tails going downwards (from the left side of the note) then three upwards (from the right of the note) – and so on (see Figure 4.2). A note on the centre line can have its tail either up or down, to complement the other notes nearby.

◼ Figure 4.2

While this piece walks along in even beats, music is not always that simple – in fact it would be pretty dull if it were! To give variety of rhythm we use differently designed notes, each showing a different duration.

In the final version of this piece the last note is a 'white' note. This is not a mistake on the composer's part! It shows that this note is to be held for the two beats needed to complete the last bar. Several types of notes are used in music, all showing the lengths of the sounds that make up the rhythm.

The notes (and their equivalent rests) that you will meet during your playing are shown in Figure 4.3.

Any further lines drawn across the tails halves their note or rest value yet again, e.g. ♪ or ♫ = 32nd notes or demi-semi-quavers but you will not need these as yet.

A 'dot' after any note increases its value by half, e.g. 𝅗𝅥· = 𝅗𝅥 + ♩; ♩· = ♩ + ♪ etc.

Any combination of notes and rests can be used as long as their total value exactly fills a bar. Play the piece again, spacing the notes the same distance apart and listening to the tune. Let it flow – sing the words if you like. The verse tells rather a sad story. Does your playing fit the mood?

piano

Note the instructions at the beginning. Music uses mainly Italian terms (sometimes also French or German) to describe how the composer wants it to be performed. A musical dictionary (obtainable from any music or book shop) will give you all you will need – and more! Speak aloud any you come across. The Italian terms are especially expressive and beautiful.

There are two more things to do to make this piece really interesting.

Notes	Rests	Count	Name	
			American	English
𝅝	▬	4	Whole note	Semibreve
𝅗𝅥 𝅗𝅥	▬	2	Half note	Minim
♩ ♩ ♩ ♩	𝄽 (or 𝄼)	1	Quarter note	Crotchet
♪♪ or ♫ ♫♫	𝄾	$\frac{1}{2}$	Eighth note	Quaver
♬♬ or ♬ ♬♬♬ ♬♬♬♬	𝄿	$\frac{1}{4}$	Sixteenth note	Semi-quaver

▪ Figure 4.3

You know the speed and mood of the music. Now punctuate it as you would the words. In music this is called **phrasing** and consists of drawing a curved line over (or under) the notes to where the comma or full stop would be in words. At the end of a phrase, and without upsetting the regular beat (or **pulse**), lift briefly off the key to allow the music to 'breathe' – much as a singer takes a quick breath between sentences.

A phrase is simply a musical sentence.

As you play, try to join all the sounds smoothly under the curved line like one long piece of string – no gaps but no overlapping blurs either. Using your new listening skills adjust the level of your wrist (it probably needs lowering a little) to pass the tune from finger to finger, relaxing into each key as you go. Make sure both keys are neither up nor down at the same time, but pass mid-way in a see-saw movement. This will produce a smooth, singing line. Practise this a few times. Don't press down hard but keep the light 'arm supported by a crane' feeling as before.

This is called *legato* playing, the opposite being *staccato* when the sounds are detached.

Finally, add marks of dynamics. Do you want the piece to be loud or soft? To stay the same all through or get louder or softer? Let's say you want it to be moderately loud (don't you want other people to hear your grumble and sympathize?) Again, Italian terms are normally used.

Some Italian terms of dynamics		
fortissimo	(abbreviated to *ff*)	very loud
forte	(abbreviated to *f*)	loud
mezzo forte	(abbreviated to *mf*)	half or moderately loud
mezzo piano	(abbreviated to *mp*)	half or moderately soft
piano	(abbreviated to *p*)	soft
pianissimo	(abbreviated to *pp*)	very soft

To get gradually softer or louder there are other Italian terms but all you need now are:

◁ or *crescendo* (cresc.) = growing gradually louder

▷ or *decrescendo* or diminuendo (dim) = growing gradually softer.

Your piece should now look like Figure 4.4.

The Pessimist

Andante dolente (fairly slowly and sadly)

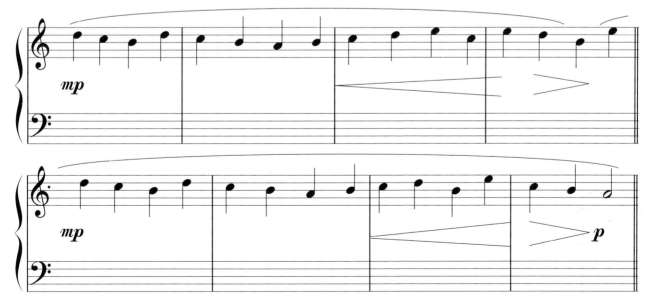

■ Figure 4.4

piano

Now imagine you are philosophical about your 'lot' in life. This second piece (Figure 4.5) has identical words and the shape looks the same but . . . !

The Optimist

Allegretto (faster than andante)

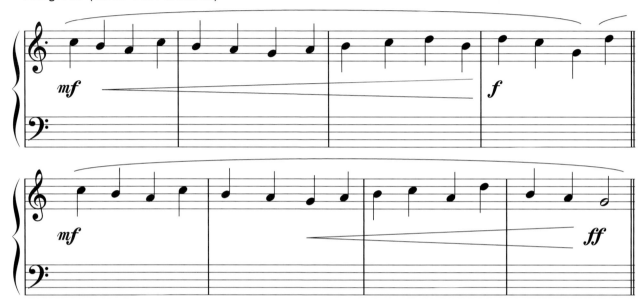

■ Figure 4.5

Hear the difference? It has a cheerful 'who cares, that's how I am!' mood but how was that achieved? Did you notice that it starts on the third space in the treble stave whereas the first piece began on the line above? Did you feel it needed to go faster, as did the composer?

Moving it one white key lower puts it into what we call the major while the first one was in the minor. It sounds quite different although the shape of the piece is virtually the same. This will be made clear later on. Meanwhile, enjoy playing it in both ways, showing the different moods.

You may not agree with the printed dynamics and phrasing. If not, GOOD FOR YOU! Experiment! Find others that you prefer. That will give you your own interpretation – and a musician's own ideas and 'colouring' of even a simple piece are part of what makes music so fascinating.

How are you getting on? If you have grasped everything so far, you are doing brilliantly!

If you have any problems go back over any sections you found difficult and try again.

If you always try to approach the keyboard as I have suggested, any current problems will right themselves as you progress.

5

Time signatures

f you have ventured into your nearest music shop to browse through the selection of tempting books – some of which you may be able to play sooner than you imagine – you will probably have noticed two numbers, one above the other, printed at the start of every piece. They appear after the clefs and before any notes and are called the **time signature** (Figure 5.1).

Figure 5.1

At first glance a time signature resembles a mathematical fraction – but take a closer look and you will see that there is no dividing line between the two numbers.

There are two kinds of time: **simple time** and **compound time** and each has its own set of time signatures. This section deals with simple time signatures.

With a simple time signature the top number shows how many full beats there are in the bar, no matter how the music's rhythm divides the beats into various note values.

The lower number tells us the kind of beat – whether we're using slow minim beats (perhaps for a funeral march), crotchet beats (for an afternoon walk) or even fast quaver beats (for a children's dance). The notes will be grouped to show the whole beats so that these are easily recognized even when they are broken up to give rhythmic variety.

Without the time signature, and faced with a variety of note values in each bar, a player could be thoroughly confused. 'How many beats, actually, are there in this bar?' 'Are they slow beats or fast ones?'

piano

While your first piece had a very basic rhythm, music would be a pretty dull affair if it always plodded along in even crotchets. To pass on to us the amazing assortment of rhythms, composers split the whole beats into a wide variety of smaller value notes and rests, giving us many beautiful and catchy rhythmic patterns (see Figure 5.2).

■ Figure 5.2

But however many notes and rests there are in a bar their total value must add up to the correct number of beats in that bar and they are usually grouped into whole beats.

Time signatures save composers from writing laboriously, 'I want to have two quarter note (♩) beats in each bar, please' or '2 × ¼ note beats' (♩ being ¼ value of a whole note, 𝅝).

He simply writes ²⁄₄ and we know exactly what he means. It is an example of composer's shorthand.

Let's say he has written a military march with two crotchet beats in a bar:

|*Left* Right |*Left* Right | ²₄ ♩ ♩ | ♪♪ ♩ | ♩ ♩ | ♩ ‖

It is an instant success and even reaches the charts. Then the King of Utopia dies and who else but our musical genius gets commissioned to write the Funeral March! Crotchet beats would be too fast for this so he chooses a slower, minim (♩) beat and writes a march with 2 × ½ beats in each bar: ²⁄₂. He also writes *largo* (very slow) in his performance directions. There can be no mistake:

|*L e f t* R i g h t |*L e f t* R i g h t | ²₂ ♩ ♩ | ♩ ♩ ♩ | ♩ ♩ | 𝅝 ‖

Similarly for three in a bar. A waltz for children could be in quaver beats: 3 × ⅛ note beats in each bar (Figure 5.3).

■ Figure 5.3

For adults a little slower 3 × ¼ note beats in each bar (Figure 5.4).

■ Figure 5.4

For elderly, plump matrons 3 × ½ note beats in each bar (Figure 5.5).

■ Figure 5.5

For four beats in a bar think of marches for various sizes of horse: Shetland pony: 4 × ⅛ note beats $\frac{4}{8}$; show jumper: 4 × ¼ note $\frac{4}{4}$; shire horse: 4 × ½ note $\frac{4}{2}$.

These different kinds of beat are vital guides to interpreting a piece.

Here is the set of simple time signatures (Figure 5.6).

(Each beat is divisible by 2 – i.e., can be halved, quartered: 'sil-ver │ ir-id-is-cent' │).

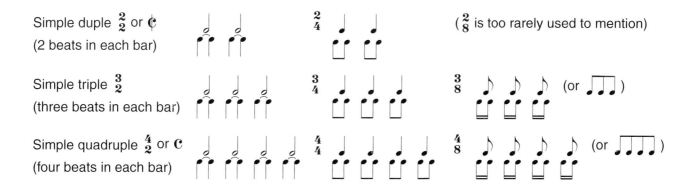

■ Figure 5.6

The C alternative to $\frac{4}{4}$ is sometimes called 'common time' but this is not correct. It is another shortcut. Similarly, the '¢' is another way of writing $\frac{2}{2}$.

Sometimes a composer wants to split a beat into three rather than two, just as a word with three syllables – 'beautiful' – might appear in a poem of mainly two-syllabled – 'lovely' – words. This is called a triplet and the three notes are grouped together with a curved line and an italic 3 over or under them. This is distinct from any finger numbering which is always printed thus: 3.

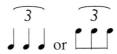

A triplet must not hold up the pulse but fit rhythmically into its beat.

6

More about legato and staccato

You met the terms *legato* and *staccato* briefly in Unit 2. Now you can discover how to recognize the signs and the best way to produce the sounds.

Legato playing

With *legato* playing you cannot know if you are getting it right unless you can hear the sounds passing smoothly from one to another so – wake up your ears!

The most usual sign of a *legato* passage is a long curved line over several notes:

To produce a good, singing *legato* you might think of a see-saw. When one end is up the other end's down. Play any key and move to the next with the see-saw action. If you listen carefully you can hear the sounds moving from one to the other without a gap or an overlap. Now play any three keys remembering that both ends of the see-saw are never up or down at the same time (unless it has been vandalized!). Listen out for blurs or gaps.

With a long *legato* passage you might think of a piece of string of the same thickness all the way and without a break. The way to practise a *legato* is to lower your arm and hand weight fractionally below keyboard level, then move from one key to the next, each finger sinking into its key as if into a comfortable arm chair. Keep your hands the right shape so that all your waiting fingertips are resting on their keys.

Slurs are short *legato* passages – often of only two or three notes. These are also linked by a short curved line. The best way to play these is to imagine your hand is a bird about to catch a fish from a lake. Swoop your hand down onto the first key, join the sounds to the end of the curved line and then 'lift off' gracefully. How deep the swoop and high the lift depends on the speed of the piece. If fast, your actions will portray a minimal picture of the bird's movements. If slow, time your swoop-and-lift gracefully.

Staccato playing

From your 'Wonky Wheel' piece you will remember that a dot *after* a note lengthens its value by half as much again. With *staccato*, dots are placed *over* or *under* notes to indicate that they are to be detached from one another – as if your long piece of string has been snipped into short, even lengths with matching gaps between them.

While there is only one sort of *legato* (you either join the sounds or you don't) there are three kinds of *staccato*.

If your *staccatos* have a curved line over them they should be played with a lazy, almost bouncy movement shortening the gaps between to about 25%:

For the second degree of staccato the sounds and following silences should be about equal in length, about 50%:

The third degree shows that the sounds are very short indeed, like pinpricks, so that the note's value has far more silence than sound. To play one of these, let your finger contact the key and flick your fingertip towards you as if you are flicking a cake crumb off the key. Make sure that you depress the key sufficiently to make the sound:

To play any *staccato* raise and lighten your arms until your hand weight is just above keyboard level. The key will then be able to return to its normal position immediately it is released.

In some long passages you will sometimes see the words: *sempre legato* or *sempre staccato*. This just means that the next passage is to be played *always smoothly* or *always detached* (*sempre* being the Italian term for *always*) and saves spotting the page with dots over every note or drawing curved lines that may need to stretch over several lines.

These are only guidelines and not rigid rules. As you progress, you will be able to judge for yourself how each should sound.

7

Warm up your fingers

M y professor, the late Sidney Harrison, often marvelled at the way we can control our fingers to produce the sounds we want.

'With our second and third we have two good strong fingers, our fourth is dependent on our third, our fifth is short, thin and weak – and our thumb goes "CLUNK".' (The gist of what he said – not a direct quote.)

Even harder, I add, is to play any finger or thumb to produce a wide variety of sounds from keys with identical mechanical actions.

So that's what we have to contend with and it never ceases to amaze me, too, that by persevering with the right sort of practice and careful listening, we can get each individual finger to make the sound we want!

Consider for a moment the different movements we make in life and how our movements vary from activity to activity – fingers for buttoning a jacket, arms for embracing a friend, whole body for digging the garden – and all the range of movements in between.

Different styles of music also need the right physical approach: minimal finger work for rapid passages, hands and arms for slower, singing phrases and whole body exertion for playing massive chords.

While a fair technique is essential for playing the piano even moderately well, I have always argued against elementary pianists spending hours of precious music time in struggling with long, complicated studies. After all, of what use is a book of brilliant technical exercises if all but the rare aspiring concert pianist cringe briefly from the first horrendous page before guiltily losing the fearsome volume down the back of the piano?

Far too much time can be wasted on these when most pianists just want to get started on playing real music – classical, romantic, jazz, blues or whatever style in our rich world of music attracts them.

That said, by spending 5–8 minutes on a few short and simple exercises at the start of your daily practice your eyes, ears and brain will become coordinated, alert and responsive when you move on to your pieces.

Before playing the first note is always a good time to check your stance at the keyboard. Poor physical positions, causing aches and even pain, are always prowling and ready to sneak in when you are concentrating on something else.

So, revise your sitting position.

Do your arms feel heavy? Are your shoulders and neck tense? Don't be tempted to 'make do' with a seat that is too high/low/hard/narrow. Find a better one to make playing so much easier. Get comfortable!

Maintaining your normal practice routine, start with any of the early finger movements you may still be finding difficult. Using both hands, play any two different fingers you decide on instantly and correctly. If you find that really easy try this:

With your eyes closed place your hands over G to D, an octave apart, and play:

1 Right hand 2–5–3 together with left hand 2–3–5, (a) loudly and (b) softly

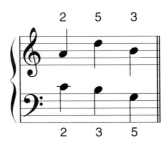

2 Left hand *staccato* 5–3–2–1 with right hand *legato* 3–5–2–3, again (a) loudly and (b) softly

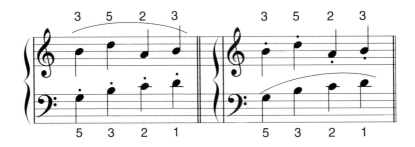

Then reverse the *staccato/legato* with each exercise. Go on to invent other progressions and develop them like these until your hand and finger independence becomes instinctive.

Now try this: Right hand move up from thumb (on G) to fifth finger (on D) using semibreves ◦ (whole notes). With these, too, vary your dynamics (louds and softs) to make the exercises more interesting (Figure 7.1).

■ Figure 7.1

Here you need a slow, heavy 'walking through mud' touch, your arms swinging your hands and fingers easily into the keys, leaving each one reluctantly as you move onto the next. Repeat with your left hand.

Now play the same thing with minims ♩ (half notes) (Figure 7.2).

■ Figure 7.2

This will be slightly faster and less heavy. Your arm movement will be less pronounced. You are 'walking' across a grassy field. Use your hand and finger weight and *listen* to match the sounds, passing evenly from sound to sound without gaps or overlaps. This is a true *legato*. Repeat with your left hand.

Now repeat the exercise using crotchets ♩ (quarter notes) (Figure 7.3).

■ Figure 7.3

piano

These move faster – fingers only, 'walking' at a brisker, lighter pace. Again, repeat with your left hand.

On to quavers ♪ ♫ (eighth notes) (Figure 7.4).

■ Figure 7.4

Quavers are generally known as 'running' notes. They sound much the same as crotchets but there are twice as many in each bar. To keep them light and fast check your hand shape and use only your fingers. Does your playing sound like running? Or merely plodding a bit faster?

Here is a very useful trick: By cutting out stresses you can make the notes sound faster while playing them at the same speed.

This is how to do it: Imagine you are standing on a path beside a wide strip of marshland and want to get to another path parallel with yours, across the marsh, without getting your feet wet. There are several firm tufts of grass about three metres apart. You decide that it will take four light steps to get from one tuft to the next.

With each hand separately play firmly into the first note; play up the next three very lightly (as if on the surface of the marsh) then the top note, which is firm, then descend again with three more light notes – and so on.

Thus, *1–2–3–4–5–4–3–2–1* (rather than *1–2–3–4–5–4–3–2–1*) gives the impression of speed even when you are not actually playing any faster.

Play the five quavers up and down several times without stopping. Aim for a swinging rhythm, up and down and try to get the 'running' sound. Repeat this with each hand separately until it feels easy, then use both hands together. Listen carefully to make sure that the sounds *are* together!

Finally, feel free to play any exercise in any way you want. Make up rhythms and play either hand as you choose. Just don't allow your hands to 'do their own thing' for that will not help you.

Persevere with these over the next few weeks – they cannot be mastered in a couple of days. Divide your practice time so that your technique and musicianship move forward together and you will soon be feeling much more in charge of your piano.

Throughout your playing, remember that it is much easier to learn a new technique with simple notes than to meet it in a difficult piece of music and have to wrestle with notes, interpretation and tricky technique all at once. So when you come across a new technique in a piece lift that bit out and turn it into an exercise before replacing it in its context.

8

Chords

C hords are made up of two or more notes played simultaneously, making one sound.

Chords can be 'concordant', that is, pleasant to listen to. Others can be very 'discordant', sounding unsettled and needing to move on to an eventually satisfying resolution.

Yet other chords may contain an assortment of notes, creating special effects, sometimes gratingly discordant that can make a listener cringe. Sometimes so beautiful that you long for them to be repeated over and over again

Each of these heavy chords

can be lightened by 'breaking' as

or   or

■ Figure 8.1

When the melody is written in the treble stave the accompanying chords in the heavier bass stave (on longer, thicker strings) would drown the melody if played with all the notes together. In order to soften that accompaniment composers can 'break' the chords into single notes to be played in any order that suits the piece (see Figure 8.1).

Look out for these chord patterns when you start learning a new piece. Recognizing them, and playing them several times as full chords, will save you the labour of learning them from single note to single note. Place your fingers over each whole chord and all you have to do is play the notes in the order in which they are written.

For special emphasis a chord can be played in 'arpeggio'. Starting with the lowest, each upward note is played rapidly in succession, all being held down together (see Figure 8.2).

■ Figure 8.2

This is suitable for a piece such as a Scottish bagpipe tune when the chord would be played loudly, as if by the drums.

When emulating the sound of a harp it would probably be played in the treble with each arpeggio soft and staccato (see Figure 8.3).

■ Figure 8.3

Practising . . . the early days

9

I f you have understood and followed everything so far you are doing really well. By revising your practice routine now you will ensure that your progress is swift and sure.

However much – or little – time you have for your daily practice, tackling it the right way can make the difference between 'muddling along' and becoming a musician.

It is not necessary to aim for professional performance standard. Almost any amateur pianist can become a fine musician provided he knows what sounds he wants to achieve, how to make them – and the ability to hear if he is doing so.

When you can play even the simplest pieces correctly, easily and beautifully you will be a musician.

Whether you have 20 minutes or an hour to spend at your piano, organize the time by dividing it into six sections:

1 Stance: Check before playing so that no part of your body will begin to ache and distract you.

2 Getting your bearings, including the leger lines.

3 Sounds: Spend a few minutes improvising and varying sound pictures. Any fingers. Any notes. Listen and adjust as necessary.

4 Technique: Check hand shape. Fingerworks. Be careful not to poke or thump the keys – even exercises can sound musical! Play each key in the same way (with the same touch) so that the sounds are matched and even and either *legato* or *staccato* as you decide. *Listen!*

5 Start learning a new piece that you think you will enjoy – but BEWARE! To amble vaguely through, making mistakes as you go, is the worst and slowest way to learn. You will simply be practising the mistakes. Your finger memory will be building up a programme of playing the wrong notes; your aural memory will pull you up short – and you will send yourself back to the beginning.

Do this a few times and the phrase will take on a whole new shape from the printed one with a squiggle (of extra wrong notes) and some 'hiccups' in the time. These will have become part of the piece. Eventually you will get frustrated and stamp off for a coffee – or something stronger.

Yes, we've all been through that – and have come to realize that it is much easier and quicker to concentrate – and play the right notes with the right fingers *every time*.

Start every new piece by playing the first phrase carefully and with the right notes and fingers, one hand at a time several times over until it is fluent and safe. If you make a slip – as we all do sometimes – go back a couple of notes and play the right ones, firmly, three or four times to fix them in your memory.

NEVER ALLOW A MISTAKE TO BECOME A HABIT.

Once a phrase is secure and shapely, move on to the next one and work in the same way. As the phrases become known let them flow a little faster until they feel 'right' for the piece. This will make more sense to your aural and finger memories.

Keen as you are to play your new piece, avoid trying to learn too much of it in any one session. Two phrases are generally enough to ensure that you will recognize them if they are repeated further down the page – as they often will be. Revise them the next day before learning two more new ones.

Notice chord patterns, recognize them even when they are 'broken'. Practise them unbroken – as whole chords – to get the feeling of the shapes and how they change from one chord to the next. Which notes move up or down? Which stay the same?

Never continue to work on one new phrase for too long. Your brain will get bored and switch off, allowing ever-prowling mistakes to creep in to wreck your day's work.

   6 Relax: Wind down by playing through any piece you already know and like.

Some days you will find practising difficult and frustrating. Persevere – and it will gradually become easier and you will be inspired again. However, to continue to struggle with a problem for too long may wreck the piece for good. Put it away until another day.

A beautiful composition may sound easy when played by an experienced pianist but, however much you would love to play it, resist the temptation if it is far beyond your stage of learning. You will come to hate everything to do with the piano! So wait until you are ready, or, if that time seems just too far ahead, visit your music shop for a simplified version – ask the manager for one that has been well harmonized as poor arrangements can render a lovely melody dull and flat.

10

Mad March

Here is another short verse:

> From the west came the whale of a gale
>
> that without 'by your leave' or 'beg pardon',
>
> blew the litter up hill and down dale
>
> and my garden all over my garden.

If you read it aloud a couple of times you will hear that the rhythm is quite different from the 'wonky wheel' ditty. This verse would sound ridiculous if forced into the same four-syllable pattern, giving it stresses on the words 'from', 'a' and 'by':

> FROM the west came | A whale of a | GALE that without | 'BY your leave' etc.

There are two things wrong with that. First, this rhythm is in threes, hence the bar lines must also be three beats apart:

> From the | WEST came a | WHALE of a | GALE etc.

Second, Mad March enters with two weak syllables leading to the first strong word, 'west'. In both poetry and music this up-beat entry is called an 'anacrusis'. In poetry the anacrusis is spoken without emphasis.

In music the anacrusis, coming before the first bar line, is also played without stress.

Here is the music that accompanies this breezy verse (Figure 10.1).

Mad March

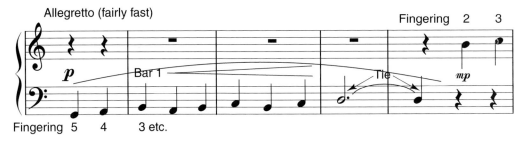

From the west came a whale of a gale _____ that with

- out 'by your leave' or 'beg par - don' _____ blew the

lit - ter up hill and down dale _____ and my

gar - den all o - ver my gar - den _____

■ Figure 10.1

It is usual to number the bars of a piece of music. This enables a player, or members of an orchestra, to find any bar that needs extra practice without wasting time. However, an anacrusis bar, being incomplete, is not included in the bar count.

Now look at the last bar. It contains only one beat because the other two were 'borrowed' for the opening anacrusis. Because it completes the number of beats this bar *is* included in the count.

Just as you would study a map before setting off on an unfamiliar journey, look through the whole piece carefully. Recognizing the shape of each phrase and how the melody rises and falls will help you to learn quickly and accurately, saving you the chore of correcting later mistakes. This applies to any new piece.

For dramatic effect the first phrase has been written entirely in the bass stave.

The second phrase moves up to the treble stave. Back to the bass for the third phrase. This is almost the same as the first phrase but it is written eight notes, one octave, higher.

Finally, to show the chaos, the last phrase weaves between your hands, all over both staves.

Now look through in more detail.

1 Can you 'hear' the shape of the music? Even at this stage, try to get some idea as to how each phrase will sound. Look at the dynamic mark, *p*, followed by a crescendo. Could this phrase be starting with a grumble of thunder and rise to a CRASH! On the top note?

2 Note where the melody switches from one hand to the other. Your ultimate aim is to keep the music flowing easily without slowing down, speeding up or changing the tone as the melody weaves between your hands. This takes practice in listening and adjusting the way you play the keys – your 'touch'.

3 Decide which finger will start each phrase. You need to place your hand over the keys so that there is a finger resting on each note that you will play.

4 Notice the rests. In music *silences* are as important as *sounds*. One note singing on beyond its given duration can ruin a harmony and 'skipping' a rest means that the next beat is reached too soon, leaving the listener feeling that he has 'missed the kerb'!

5 While one-count (crotchet) rests are used to make up the part-bars, four-count (semibreve) rests have been written for the wholly silent bars.

Working on parchment with quill pen and ink – as many of the greatest composers had to – was a time-consuming chore when these musical geniuses were desperate to write down their fleeting inspirations. Hence they worked out several gems of musical shorthand to save time and effort. This is one of them.

One short mark, (a four-beat rest) scratched along the underside of the fourth line, showed that that bar was to be silent for that hand (or instrument in the case of an orchestral piece). This was far quicker than painstakingly drawing a separate rest for every silent beat.

Hence this 4–beat rest simply shows that, *no matter whether the piece is in duple, triple or quadruple time, that whole bar is meant to be silent*. A completely empty bar might make the player wonder if the composer had forgotten to write notes in it!

Gradually, over the centuries, many invaluable morsels of musical shorthand evolved and are now accepted symbols in our musical notation.

6 At the end of each phrase, in bars 3, 7, and 11, is a short curved line linking the dotted minim (3–beat note) to the crotchet in the following bar. This is not a phrase line because it curves across the bar line *to the same note* in the following bar. It means that the composer wants the dotted minim to sing on for a fourth beat, beyond the end of the bar. Obviously, four beats cannot be squeezed into a bar that is designed to hold three. Hence, it has to 'overflow' into the next bar – just as four glasses of milk would overflow – somewhat more messily – if you poured them into a jug that would hold only three. This curved line, which is strictly from one note to an identical note, with no other notes in between, is called a 'tie'. Both notes are counted but only the dotted minim is played, the following tied crotchet being held down for its value but not played again.

There is a new sign at the end of the third phrase, ⌢ . This indicates a pause and simply means that the note is held down for its full value, plus a stretching on of the sound while you say 'p-a-u-s-e' to yourself. This does two things. It warns the listener (1) that it is nearly the end so get ready to clap or (2) if the piece doesn't sound as if it is coming to an end, the 'pause' creates suspense. What's coming next?

The short time given to this pre-playing work applies to every new piece and will always help you to learn quickly and accurately, saving you much of the tedious chore of correcting mistakes later.

You have been very patient! At last it is time for you to play.

First phrase: Lift your left hand onto the keyboard and place the fingers lightly over their five notes, first playing them silently to feel the shape of the phrase. Lift your hand off the keyboard for the 'rests' in bar 4:

Fingering: 5–4– | **3**–4–3 | –**2**–3–2– | 1 – hold – hold | hold – rest – rest |

Now play the notes, 'thinking' towards the first beat of each bar so that the triple rhythm emerges. Starting *piano* (***p***) (softly), gradually *crescendo* (become louder) to imitate the rising grumble of thunder and end *forte* (***f***) (loudly). Your strong thumb will have no difficulty with that! Hold that note down, counting its value evenly. Keep the phrase very *legato* (smooth) – you will need to practise this phrase several times to improve the *legato* line you achieved with your first piece. Play the whole phrase through a few times until it begins to feel fluent.

Second phrase: The right hand enters with a nervous little narration before the left hand pushes it out with a strong gust of wind. Play this ***parlando*** (in a conversational style). It is not difficult but be aware that keys (and fingers) are 'skipped' where there are no notes on those lines or spaces. Try to get it right every time to avoid having to correct it later.

Third phrase: Here the left hand returns, an octave (eight notes) higher than before. The melody climbs straight up *six* notes – but you have only five fingers! Your second finger has to 'pop' over your thumb and play the top note exactly on the beat – and then return to its normal position in time to play again. Don't allow your hand to stiffen – practise 'flipping' your second finger easily over and back a few times.

This sixth note actually belongs in the treble stave (the first line, 'E') but playing the whole phrase with the left hand makes for a far smoother shape than if it were split between both hands. Thus, when the note is to be played as part of your left hand's phrase, it is written as you see.

Fourth phrase: This phrase is simply chaos. It is not as straightforward as the other phrases and you will need to spend more time on it. The melody tumbles about between your hands to show the chaos of flower pots, seed trays and bits of trees blowing about all over your garden.

Play it through a couple of times. In music, as in so many things we do, there are nearly always patches that are trickier to play than the rest. Always lift these out and work on each until it is fluent, then build up the speed so that it flows as freely as the rest of the piece.

Think of music's tricky bits as tough patches of grass on a lawn you are mowing, or spilled wine on a carpet you are cleaning. These places need working over several times to get a good overall result – but would you mow the whole lawn over and over again, just to remove the bit of tough grass, or clean the whole carpet as many times as the patch with the stain on it?

It is the same with music. If you habitually start at the beginning of your piece and play it straight through every time, the tricky bits will not go away. You will always stumble or hesitate in the same places and the mistakes will eventually become habits and normal parts of the piece. So take these rough patches out and give them extra time and practice.

As soon as you have done your technical warm-ups work on any tricky bits in your pieces before you tire and your concentration wanes. These awkward passages can often be the most interesting and beautiful to play so give them enough time, thought and practice to bring them up to the same standard as the whole piece.

This approach will eventually give you the satisfaction of being able to play your pieces, all through, just as you want them to be.

In this piece you will probably have decided that the last line is the one needing extra care. Without sounding any notes first 'mime' the weaving movements of your hands above the keyboard.

Then begin with the last note – and work backwards. Having played the last note to your satisfaction, start the next note back and run into the last. Then three notes back, running through to the end. Repeat two or three times until it flows easily.

Now move back to the three previous bass notes and run them to the end a few times. Then the three treble notes at the beginning of the line. Eventually you will be able to weave the whole line easily and evenly between the hands.

'Working backwards' is an excellent way to practise the harder sections of any piece, for instead of continually (and depressingly) coming to a wall of strange ideas, you will be 'steering your ship from stormy seas into a safe and familiar harbour'. You will always work towards the part you know.

One of the most satisfying aspects of practice is suddenly finding that you have completely erased the tricky bits and they are indistinguishable from the rest.

One word of caution.

Even when they know a piece really well some people are terrified of 'letting go'. They can't bring themselves to trust their automatic finger memory (in the muscles of the fingers) to take over and are always worrying in case they play wrong notes instead of revelling in their performance. They are like babies, watching every step they take and are sure to fall over before long.

Far from producing a perfect result, this approach only makes for wandering concentration, mistakes in different places every time and frustration.

Compare very cautious playing with riding a bicycle at a slow walking pace. And a memorized poem would be both hard to remember and dreary to listen to if recited in a slow drone.

At this stage you are naturally still a little anxious but as soon as even one phrase is secure have courage and try 'letting go'. Once you know a piece well remember that it is better to play the *wrong notes in the right way than the right notes in the wrong way*. So let the music move along easily – and enjoy it!

You will notice that I often use the word 'easy'. Haven't you watched Wimbledon tennis players, Olympic diving champions or even circus trapeze artists and thought: 'That looks so easy I'm sure I could do it'?

However talented, without a background of regular practice none of them could achieve their fine performance.

And when you find a whole piece is easy and fun to play *you* will be playing it really well!

Learning a new piece needs concentration so do not try to do too much at any one practice. Spending too long on anything will bore you and you will start making silly and infuriating mistakes. We all do it sometimes! So remember, there is always tomorrow. Leave it and go on to something else.

When you can play the whole piece easily check the dynamics (the 'louds' and 'softs' of the music). Listen acutely. Does it sound as you wanted, getting louder or softer as you meant it to? If in doubt, experiment to see how you prefer the phrases to sound. You may like to play them differently each day to give them other interpretations. It is up to you!

11

How to show a passage is to be repeated

L et us suppose you are a poverty-stricken musician, living in one unheated room without any of the tools of a professional composer. You have only a few precious sheets of manuscript paper, a quill pen and bottle of ink – and your genius!

At last your hunger has inspired a really magical piece but it is 16 pages long and writing it down is proving extremely tedious. Furthermore, you are fast running out of manuscript paper. If only you didn't have to keep rewriting all those sections that you want to be repeated it would all be so much easier!

Gazing round the littered room you notice some scruffy notes on the theory of music, left by the previous tenant. It is half hidden under an old pizza carton (or the 15th-century equivalent) and by chance the top page shows drawings of signs you haven't met before:

'Eureka!' you yell (or the 15th-century equivalent). Without cutting a moment off the performance of your magnificent work you have discovered how to cut the writing-out time – and the consumption of manuscript paper – to less than half.

With 𝄆, an easy-to-write sign at the start of the passage to be repeated and 𝄇 at the end of that passage, you can instruct the performer to 'play the bit between those signs again' without your having to copy it all out. Even better, if the player is to repeat from the very beginning, you only need to draw the 𝄇 part of the sign!

Should you want the player to go back over a less easily identifiable section you can write '**DS**' (***dal segno***) – from the sign, 𝄋 written wherever you want the repeat to begin.

DC (***da capo***) – from the start – speaks for itself.

Finally, in songs with several verses you can show how many times you want the verses, usually the chorus, to be repeated:

Blessing the previous tenant for his inventiveness (brought on by necessity) you conclude your spectacular – pop song? (for that's where the money is!) with a short *coda*, or 'tail piece' and set off on the long trudge to take it to your publisher, the prospects of fame and fortune speeding your bare feet on the icy pavements.

| 1⌉ | 2⌉ | 3 ⌉ |

Well, not quite. But now you know what these signs mean!

Getting a melody to sing over the accompaniment

There can be little more teeth gritting to a musician than the sound of a beautiful melody being swamped by an over-heavy bass.

You already know that the bass strings are longer – and the lowest ones thicker – than the treble ones, giving out strong, deep sounds. To allow their beautiful melody to sing above this composers often resorted to 'breaking' their heavy chords. (See Unit 8.)

Even then it is almost impossible for a beginner to balance his hands so that the melody will sing exquisitely over an often dull accompanying bass.

This lack of balance is the hallmark of many amateur pianists – but anyone can lift their playing out of that status.

Here is the trick that will give your playing the professional 'touch' of making one hand sing and shape a melody at the same time as the other plays a soft accompaniment.

It is simply a matter of teaching another technique to our old friend, coordination.

First, select a phrase that needs this adjustment:

1 Play the RH alone, concentrating on getting a lovely singing tone, perhaps a little louder than you will eventually play it. Repeat several times.

2 Repeat the phrase – but this time 'play' the LH accompaniment on your knee. Listen – did you alter the melody line in any way? When you are happy with that, move on.

3 Repeat the RH phrase yet again, this time playing the LH accompaniment *silently* on the correct keys. Again, listen carefully. Your melody should still have its original, beautiful shape.

4 Repeat the phrase once more, this time play the accompaniment, very softly, on the keyboard.

LISTEN! Has your melody faltered? Has it lost its tone? If so, return to 1 and try again.

Here is a phrase for you to try (see Figure 12.1).

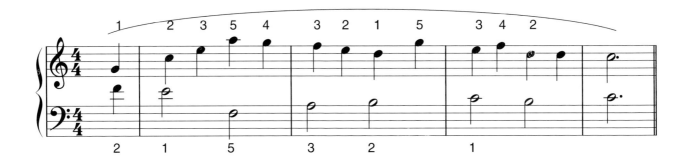

Figure 12.1

Now reverse the procedure, giving your LH a melody and keeping your RH softly controlled, for a beautiful bass melody can be shattered by a shrill treble accompaniment (see Figure 12.2).

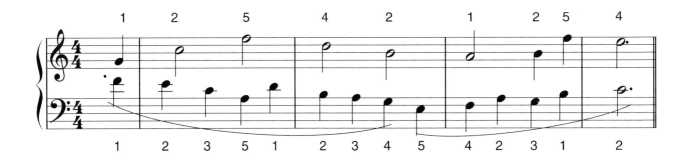

■ Figure 12.2

Add this to the technique section of your daily practice and you will be amazed to find that, after a week or so, this initially difficult skill has become easy and automatic.

Later you can adjust the dynamic 'space' between melody and accompaniment but for now you can rejoice that your coordination has vastly improved and your hands are becoming wonderfully independent of each other!

As soon as you can, use this trick in your playing. First, play the wrong way (with both hands using the same weight) then use your new skill – and listen to the difference! Does it sound good? Well done! You have mastered one of piano-playing's toughest techniques! Give yourself a hearty pat on the back!

Practising . . . when you are ready

The quickest way to learn a piece and play it beautifully is by practising in the right way. However little piano time you can manage *organize* your practice.

Always start by checking your stance so that no part of your body will begin to ache and distract you from what you are trying to achieve. Then divide your time into five approximate parts:

1 Technique: Warming up your fingers, getting them to coordinate with your brain and getting both 'into gear'   25% of your time

2 New piece: Needs single-minded concentration and is tiring so only   20%

3 Polishing last learned piece: Lift out and work the tricky bits first   30%

4 Exploring: See 5   15%

5 Your 'repertoire': Reward yourself by playing your old favourites. You worked hard to learn them so don't let them fall into decay. It is always good to have a store of pieces you can play to friends or simply for yourself to enjoy   10%.

Finally, it is said that an amateur practises until he gets it right but a professional practises until it *never goes wrong*. That should be every pianist's aim, whatever his standard.

14

Sharps, flats and naturals

You have long since been able to find your way confidently about the keyboard by the white keys, A–G. Now open the top lid of your piano again and play every white key from C to B. As you do so watch the hammers and you will see that, although the seven you played struck their strings, there were five more that were not used.

These five hammers, and their strings and dampers, belong to the black keys, each of which we call 'sharp' or 'flat', depending on whether we approach it from above or below the white key we are using.

The shortest distance from any one key to its neighbour, black or white, up or down, is called a 'semitone'.

If you sat on something *sharp* you would stand *up*. In music, a sharp sign ♯ before a note means that you play it one *semitone up* from the written note to either the next black or white one.

Likewise, if you are feeling *flat* you are probably rather *down*. The musical sign for a flat is ♭ and means that you play the note one *semitone down* – again it may be either black or white.

Music also uses 'double sharps' 𝄪 and 'double flats' ♭♭. This simply means that you play the note up or down two semitones (one tone) from the line or space it is written on but you will not meet that for some time.

If a composer wants to dispense with any sharp or flat he uses a natural sign: ♮. A double sharp or double flat that he wants to return to single sharp or flat is printed ♮♯ or ♮♭.

Play the D key, anywhere on the keyboard. Now play the key one *semitone* up. This black key is D sharp. But if you play the E key, then move to the black key one semitone down, what was D sharp is now E flat! This time you approached it from above and 'flattened' it.

Some white keys, too, have two names. You can move from E to E sharp (usually F) or from F to F flat (usually E). Likewise with B and C.

Any added sharps, flats or naturals that are not in the **Key** (see Unit 19) of the piece are called accidentals. Unless contradicted, accidentals only last throughout the bar they are written in and affect every note on that line or space throughout that bar. The following bar line 'erases' the accidental, the notes then reverting to their normal positions.

Think about style

A pianist's technique may be enviable. Fingers sparkling up and down the keyboard with never a wrong note let alone a 'split' one (where a finger accidentally squashes two keys together, smudging the sound). The audience holds its breath in admiration. What skill! Such brilliance!

But as the recital continues a certain restlessness comes over the listeners. They are looking at their programmes. 'Lullaby' by Frederick Chopin. Isn't a lullaby soft and caressing? Apart from the opening phrases, once the slow melody line shatters into switchbacks of rapid notes it sounds exactly like the first piece – brilliant and sharp! Oh well, perhaps baby's been naughty or mother's cross. What's next?

Ah! Brahms' piano pieces Opus 117. Of all the melodious themes and thick, warm harmonies, his rank among the finest. The pianist can't go wrong with these – can he? Well. Even though he managed a few early bars of rather beautiful phrasing the same touch hardened the liquid passages like broken glass.

I am not exaggerating. I have heard concert pianists playing all styles of music as if written by one composer for the identical instrument. They sounded the way tinned soup tastes: the same whether chicken, mushroom, even leek and potato.

It is usual for beginners to play everything in the same way. Later it will only need a little pre-play thought to get in the mood of each piece and develop different 'touches' – softly caressing the keys for a love song; strongly regular for a military polonaise; easy going for an amble through the fields.

Even the same type of dance can have different interpretations. Take a waltz. Always three beats in a bar but a modern ballroom waltz is graceful and flowing whereas you need a quite different approach for a 15th-century waltz. Think of the clothes people wore in those days. Tiny silk slippers and tightly waisted dresses for the ladies. For their partners? Silver buckled shoes and shirts adorned with flouncy lace. High wigs for both. Male ballroom dancers would wear black evening dress. Their ladies? A long, full, softly flowing gown designed for swirling.

So a pianist needs to become an impressionist, 'donning the hat' of each composer before sitting at the piano. Then the 'lift on, lift off' gives time for 'becoming' Mozart or Fats Waller. Always keep the picture in mind and think in the mood and style, even while you are still getting to grips with the music.

Revise a piece – a march would be best – that you know really well.

Now change it. Play it as if for a grand parade. Change it again – for small children's dance class, a tip-toe march. Now it is early morning and everyone else is asleep, how softly can you play it? Now as if you are accompanying an old black and white movie called 'When the Bars Closed' featuring Laurel and Hardy.

All these are totally different styles and, as an exercise, you might like to try this with any of your pieces. Have fun!

16

Exploring

Look back to not so long ago when you sat at your piano without any idea of how to play it. You didn't know one note from another. You poked nervously at a key – and were surprised that it sounded – or didn't if your touch was too light. If you managed to pick out a tune you played it with one finger. You had no skills. All you had then were excitement, expectation and determination. And haven't they done you well! Now everything you play makes musical sense. Your fingers are your obedient servants – well trained and obliging.

You are on the way to becoming a musician and you have done brilliantly. It's time to acquire a new, special and extremely valuable skill. The ability to play music reasonably well without having to learn it. A very few people seem to be able to do this almost instinctively but most of us have to work at it.

Think of this as exploring a wide variety of music just for the pleasure of trying out new styles and composers. It can be likened to skimming the pages of a library book before deciding whether or not to borrow it. Does anyone actually *learn* the library book first? Of course not! You are now going to sample music in the same way, running through it to get the idea of what the piece is about. If you become a keen explorer you will always have music you've borrowed or bought stacked up waiting to be tried out.

Devote 15 per cent of your practice time to exploring. Until you become proficient choose music that is much easier than the pieces you are currently learning for you will be aiming to play them straight through, without stopping, to grasp the essence and character.

Bringing 'exploring' regularly into your piano time will mean that learning new music gradually becomes much easier. Later, being able to play anything (within reason) that is put before you, getting it to sound roughly as it should, you will be especially valuable as an accompanist for a friendly sing-song, carols or at a spontaneous musical get-together. That stage won't happen in a week or two – or even in a couple of years. Nevertheless, every time you try to make sense of a previously unseen piece of music you will be taking another step towards being able to play most pieces at first sight almost as easily as if you had practised them.

Open your music and check your stance. Look through the music as if you are about to learn it.

Then check:

How will you play it? (like a march/dance/lively etc.)

Where will you play it? (clefs – treble? bass?)

Are there any sharps or flats to remember?

What time is it in? (duple? triple? quadruple? keep a very steady, even pulse)

Look through (noting phrasing, fingering etc.)

Play straight through as firmly and steadily as you can

Exploring is the one time you can be – in fact, must be – a 'hit and run driver'. When you make a mistake – as every explorer does – leave it metaphorically 'lying in the gutter'. Play on, without hesitating, keeping in strict time. This is one time when a metronome (see Unit 18) is invaluable for making you keep on playing.

When an orchestra first tries out a new work every member will make dozens of mistakes. If each individual stopped and corrected his latest error the whole structure would fall apart. By keeping in time – even by skipping that bar and coming in again at the next one – everyone gets some idea of the shape and meaning and their next run-through will begin to sound more like the composer intended.

So when exploring KEEP GOING AT ALL COSTS. Start at a slower pace than the piece should be played and you will not be forced to stop and pick yourself up.

If you have mastered your very first brain/finger coordination exercise (Unit 2) you should have no difficulty in exploring new pieces without lowering your eyes from the music. Just as a touch-typist works without watching his hands so your own fingers should play without being checked up on.

Persevere with this and you will eventually be able to pick up much of the easier and popular music and play it straight through.

17

Accents – and a composer's tale

To accent a note you need to strike the key swiftly and with some force. This produces a suddenly loud sound in a phrase of softer ones.

When accents are needed special marks are printed over the relevant notes:

This is struck and sustained

This, accented during a run

This, sharply *staccato*

(But there are no fast rules about these, just play them in context, as you decide.)

In middle Europe during the 18th century many noblemen employed their own composer/conductor and a band of eight musicians (usually four string and four wind players) as a normal part of their household.

Musicians of that time had pianos with good dynamic range (as opposed to the mono-dynamic sounds of the earlier plucked string instruments) and often used tricks to keep their well-fed and wined audience awake. Accents, pauses, sudden changes of dynamics or tempo were introduced – sometimes a whole bar of silence followed by a crashing chord followed by a melody so beautiful that hearts broke and tears flowed. For even the shortest dull section would set everyone in the hall nodding off.

Imagine you live in Vienna in 1764 and have been invited to a grand party given by Prince Nicholas Esterhazy. The Prince is well known for his musical extravaganzas – after all, besides the magnificent pre-concert banquets he has one of the finest composers around, Joseph Haydn, among his musicians and has even built his own concert hall!

Slightly nervous, you have accepted the invitation.

The great day arrives. It has not been a good one. It is mid-winter and you have been standing at a desk in an unheated office since eight o'clock that morning. At six o'clock you hurry home, change for the party, struggle out again through the snow – and are ushered into a bright banqueting hall.

There is a blazing log fire at each end and a row of sparkling chandeliers across the ornate ceiling. All along one side are tables laden with luxury foods of every kind and enough wine punch to flood the whole town.

You eat and drink your fill. Then liveried footmen usher you and the other guests into the concert hall, where comfortable chairs have been lined up. You and the other guests are expected to sit and listen to music specially composed for the occasion.

You settle into your chair and . . .

This is where Haydn and his musicians have to keep every guest so entranced that all are still sitting upright and alert as the last chord is played. If he fails and Prince Esterhazy is confronted with rows of snoring guests, Haydn and the band may well be sacked.

What you don't know is that Haydn is fed up. All year the audience has been made up of local people, few of whom are particularly musical and many who only attend for the refreshments.

Gradually, the routine of composing for party after dull party has drained Haydn and he can feel his inspiration failing. He is, in fact, exhausted. He has become so tired and bored that he is finding it difficult to come up with new and exciting music for every occasion and two months ago he asked Prince Nicholas to let him and his weary musicians take a holiday. The Prince had readily given his permission but had asked Haydn to compose for just three more pre-arranged occasions. Haydn reluctantly agreed – but the Prince forgot and planned still more parties.

Even though the band appreciated their luck, both in their luxurious surroundings and in having such a gifted composer to conduct them, they, too, were becoming stale and irritable.

Nowadays musicians would probably go on strike, but Haydn is too clever for that. He appreciates his good fortune in having one of the best jobs around and doesn't want to risk losing it. So he has composed a unique symphony – with a twist in its tail!

And you, sitting in the audience, are about to hear it!

Haydn has secretly instructed his players to perform the first three movements of his symphony as usual. But during the final movement, instead of sitting quietly when each part comes to an end, every player in turn is to stand up, pack his instrument into its case, put on his coat and, none too quietly, walk off the platform.

Eventually only the first violin and Haydn are left and ignoring the applause, they too wander off the platform!

You and the rest of the audience roar your appreciation with a standing ovation while Prince Nicholas just smiles ruefully as he takes the hint. Next week the musicians really will get their holiday.

Today that work has become known as Haydn's 'Farewell' Symphony.

His Surprise Symphony is another example of his tremendous sense of fun. Picture him gleefully lulling his audience almost to sleep with a gentle, rocking melody – then suddenly waking them with a huge CRASH!!!

These two symphonies are still performed. Seek out a concert with them in the programme so you can enjoy them too.

Haydn was well known for his practical jokes and sense of humour but he still managed to catch people out – even with his music.

And what *music* we have inherited from those times!

The next time you learn a piece break away from the printed page and add some pauses, accents or whatever you like and see how many ways you can bring the 'notes' to life.

18

The metronome

A metronome is a mechanical aid to keeping a regular beat, or pulse. It usually relies on being wound with a key (like a clock) and is often used by composers to indicate the speed they want their work to be played.

disc Traditional metronomes are pyramid shaped with upright pendulums that, by means of a sliding weight, can be set to 'tick' at any speed from 42 to 200 a minute. They have either a plastic or wooden casing but are quite fragile and one 'drop' is usually enough to break them – often irreparably.

Some metronomes have a bell that 'tings' on any beat of a bar at the player's decision – a very useful practising aid for players with a wavery sense of pulse but not to be used continuously. Only marches and some dances keep strictly in time, all other music is quite 'elastic' with a natural 'give' and too rigid a pulse can make it sound mechanical and dull.

Nowadays, there are other types of metronomes. Some are electronic with a light that can be set to blink on the beat. Others are flat and neat like pocket calculators.

Some metronomes, especially the older type, have Italian terms of speed printed inside the metronome. Ignore these! They are meaningless as the speed depends entirely on the *kind* of beat you are using – quaver – crotchet – minim etc.

When a piece can be given two or three interpretations by being played at different speeds, the composer usually writes a metronome mark above the first bar of a piece to show which he wants, e.g.:

(metronome mark) ♩ = 138 or ♩ = 69

With the traditional type of metronome the player slides the weight up or down the pendulum on to that number, sets it swinging and listens to 'feel' the beat of the quaver, minim or whatever before starting to play.

However, while a metronome mark can be a useful guide it need never be slavishly obeyed. It makes no sense to try to play at the MM speed if it is so fast that your performance suffers. You may decide that you prefer the piece at a slower, or faster, pace than the metronome mark dictates. You are free to do so – but do try out the printed tempo as well as your own.

As we become familiar with a piece we often change our minds about the interpretation so always choose a speed (**tempo**) that enables you to get the sounds you want.

Most music shops sell a variety of metronomes at a range of prices. It is up to you whether you prefer one with a 'tinger', a 'beeper' or a 'blinker'.

Metronomes are not essential to learning to play the piano but most beginners occasionally have problems in keeping a regular pulse – and even advanced players often need to use one!

19

The other sort of key

In almost any language some words have more than one meaning – e.g. 'bustle' = a frame under a lady's skirt or 'bustle' = busily rushing about. Most dictionaries give around 16 meanings for the little word 'key' and at least two of them refer to music.

As you already know, one of the meanings concerns the black and white piano keys. It is now time to understand about the other musical meaning of Key (to avoid confusion I will use a capital K for his meaning). This is a little more complicated so sit at the piano and give yourself more time than usual.

This second meaning of Key is the addition of sharps, ♯, or flats, ♭, that a composer uses to show the player which scale he has chosen for writing his piece.

A scale is an alphabetical succession of sounds, going up or down from a starting note to its octave.

disc There are three kinds of scale in general use today: major scales, minor scales and chromatic scales. You already know that the distance from any piano key to the next one, up or down, black or white, is called a semitone. 'Semi' means 'half' and it follows that two semitones equal one *tone*.

If you count every *semitone* between a key and its same letter-named key, one octave up or down, you will find there are 12.

Scales are made up of regular patterns of these tones and semitones. Every major scale uses the same arrangement of eight of them; minor scales use them in a slightly different arrangement. I will deal with the major scale first.

Here is the pattern of tones and semitones of the scale of C major:

C (tone to) D (tone to) E (semitone to) F

then a linking tone to

G (tone to) A (tone to) B (semitone to) C

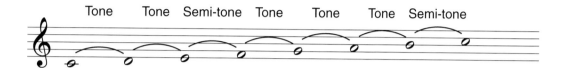

Any piece using these notes (in any order chosen by the composer for his melody or accompaniment) is said to be 'in the Key of C' (with major Keys we usually drop the word 'major'). If you start on B and play only the white keys up to the next B, it will not sound anything like the scale of C because the tones and semitones fall in a different order.

Count up from C (as your first key) to the fifth key, G, and play the scale of G major, following the major scale's pattern of tones and semitones. You will find that it has all the same white notes as C – *until you reach the seventh, F.* To maintain the pattern – and imitate the sound – you need a semitone between the F and the top G so you must raise the F to F♯. That scale is now 'the scale of G major' and any piece using those notes would be 'in the Key of G'.

To remind players that every F in the piece must be raised a ♯ is printed immediately after the clefs and before the time signature. This is called the **Key signature**:

Now move up five keys from G to D and play the D major scale. The first four keys will be the same as G major (don't forget the F♯) and you must again raise the seventh key to C♯ to keep the semitone from seventh to eighth keys. Here is the Key signature for the scale of D:

If you continue to build like this you will see that the sharp keys progress from 0 sharps (C major) through the Keys of G, D, A, E, B and F# major, each adding one more sharp in the Key signature.

There can be from 0 sharps or flats, up to six of either – *never* a mixture of both – in a Key signature and they are always written in the order they arise: F#, C#, G# etc. Unlike the time signature that appears only once, the clefs and Key signatures are repeated at the start of every line of music to remind players where to play and what scale the piece has been written in.

If you want to know which Key a piece has been written in, you only need to look at the last sharp to have been added in the Key signature – they are always written in the same order – and the next semitone up is your Key note (scale-name note).

Starting with C major play three or four sharp scales in sequence.

With 12 semitones, each having a scale, that number of sharps would half fill the stave! To dodge that problem we bring in the flat keys. Major flat keys have the identical pattern of tones and semitones as the sharp keys but this time, again starting on C, climb up only *four* keys to F.

To keep to the tone–semitone pattern you will find that the fourth note, B, has to be one semitone lower, that is, a ♭ is placed on the B line after the clef to show that every B in the piece is to be flattened. That scale is now 'in the Key of F'.

To find the Key with two flats, start on the first flat (B♭) and, again, climb up to lower (flatten) the fourth key, E♭. Any piece using the notes of that scale is 'in the Key of B♭'. To find subsequent flat keys continue climbing four keys up from the last flat.

Starting with C major play three or four flat keys in sequence.

This may all seem rather tedious but if there were no Key signature to remind you which notes were to be sharpened or flattened, the sharps and flats would have to be added in front of every note to be affected – making the page very black and messy! As it is, only accidentals – extra sharps, flats or naturals outside the scale – are written in wherever they occur.

You may wonder why we need so many Keys and why all music cannot simply be written in the Key of C. The answer is that, if that were so, music would be very boring to listen to!

Think of Keys as houses. Spending our entire lives in one room, never going out – even into the garden, never seeing another person – would send most of us, well, crackers with boredom! Coffee with a neighbour, walking the dog – even a shopping trip – livens up any day.

The design of your neighbour's house might be identical to yours but her taste in wallpaper, her furnishings, her pictures are different from yours; the countryside is ever changing; even the supermarket has a variety of displays according to the current promotion or the time of year.

So it is with keys. Later you may be able to hear that a piece in one Key sounds like warm brown velvet while another Key renders it a more cheerful yellow.

You wear clothes? They may be all the same size but you surely have a range of colours, styles and textures for different occasions.

Composers often have favourite Keys too – they feel that their music sounds better in a flat – or sharp – Key, some even changing Key during the piece, thus making their works wonderfully colourful and varied, simply because they are using different Keys for different moods. Remember Haydn and his struggles to keep his audience awake in Unit 17? Choosing the Key to suit the mood of each piece was something he knew all about!

Look back to your first piece, the 'wonky wheel'.

There were two versions of the same tune, the first sad, the second cheerful and I promised you I'd explain later how, by simply moving the tune down one note, I changed the mood. Now you can see that that was because I used a different pattern of tones and semitones.

The second version ('The Optimist') was bright and cheerful and was written using the pattern of a major scale and was therefore in a major Key.

The first ('The Pessimist') needed to be muted and sad and used the tone–semitone pattern of a minor scale. The piece is in a minor Key.

There are two types of minor scales – harmonic and melodic. Here I will only touch briefly on the harmonic minors.

Each of the 12 harmonic minor scales also has an identical tone–semitone pattern, different from its major scale in that the third and the sixth notes are flattened (lowered) by one semitone. (All minor scales have different Key signatures from the majors but you will not need to know about that yet.)

⊙ Take the scale of C minor:

C (tone to) D (semitone to) E♭ (tone to) F

(tone to) G (semitone to) A♭ (tone and a half to) B (semitone to) C

You will see that only two notes have been altered to make this lovely scale – the third, E, and the sixth, A, have both been 'flattened', creating a beautiful sound between the A♭ and the B♮.

Play the harmonic minor scale of C – and enjoy its tragic beauty.

Figure 19.1 shows the major Keys up to four sharps or four flats. You will not need any others for a while.

Sharp key signatures (major keys)

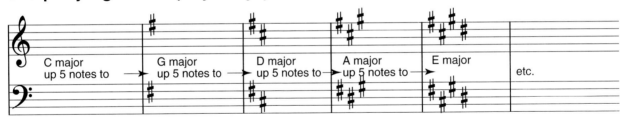

C major
up 5 notes to →   G major
up 5 notes to →   D major
up 5 notes to →   A major
up 5 notes to →   E major   →   etc.

Flat key signatures (major keys)

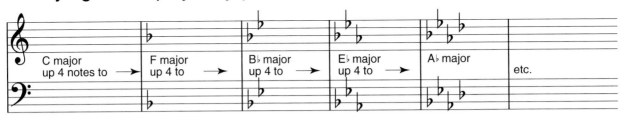

C major
up 4 notes to →   F major
up 4 to →   B♭ major
up 4 to →   E♭ major
up 4 to →   A♭ major   →   etc.

■ Figure 19.1

The chromatic scale, using all 12 semitones, is easily recognizable by its many accidentals. It is easy to play by placing your third finger over each black key and your thumb on every white key, adding your second finger to 'help out' when there are two adjacent white keys. Whichever note you start on, the pattern is always the same.

A chromatic scale:

20

Organize your fingers

As you have discovered, while there are piano keys to left and right almost as far as you can reach, you have only five fingers on each hand to play them with.

Now that you understand all about scales seems a good time to give you a few hints about playing them easily and fluently. A lot of piano music contains scale passages – often quite long ones – that are the downfall of many otherwise musically competent pianists. This can be because their technique is not good enough. Their stance may be poor – raised shoulders/slouched back. These could inhibit their hand positions so that their fingers are not able to work freely.

Most likely their fingering is haphazard, disorganized and changes every time they play those passages. There is no security of habit when they most need it – at the moment of performance. Initially, they may have been so eager to play the piece that they didn't bother to isolate the tricky bits and work out the best fingering for them. Neither have they practised them out of context. Now they're upset to hear something's wrong and frustrated because they don't know how to put it right!

Starting from scratch there is a neat and easy trick to fool your listener into thinking that you have as many fingers as there are piano keys. Amazingly few amateur pianists know how to do it.

Consider your scale of C major. One octave uses eight keys but counting your thumb you have only five fingers. How are you going to play that without a break or a bump? First, check your stance and make sure that your hand is still the beautifully curved shape of your tabletop days before your piano arrived.

Start with your RH thumb on C and play up – er – your five fingers? – no, you've run out already. Try again. Play up *three* fingers, slip your thumb under the curve of your hand to play the fourth key, reposition your fingers over the five remaining keys and continue up to top C. Was there a suspicion of a break in the *legato*? Or a bump when your thumb hit the fourth key?

The trick is to begin moving your thumb towards its next key (F) as soon as it has passed the sound to the second finger (D). By the time your third finger plays your thumb will already be hovering over the

F key. Play it to match the other sounds and climb on up to C. Your wrist needs to be flexible to swing your hand to cover the top keys:

1–2–3–1–2–3–4–5 Come down in reverse: 5–4–3–2–1–3–2–1

Being a mirror image of your RH your LH will start with fifth finger on C and move up to thumb on G before slipping third finger discreetly over thumb to play A. It follows that, descending, it will use the fingering of the RH ascending. You may find this easier if you play both thumbs together on middle C and move out and back (in 'contrary motion'):

LH   RH

5–4–3–2–1–3–2–1   1–2–3–1–2–3–4–5

That is really all there is to it but you would be amazed to see how many people stick their thumb out stiffly – in the opposite direction to where it needs to go! Then they have to rush it back to reach its new key, invariably with a bump.

Now play the scale of F. This, of course, has a flattened fourth note – B♭. Playing a black key with your short thumb is quite awkward so here you need to use thumb, then second, third and fourth on B♭, and then thumb, *that has been moving under your hand towards its next key*. Let your fingers 'walk' your hand forward a little so your fourth finger needn't stretch out to play the B♭.

Often a passage begins on a black key – sometimes being followed by a second and even a third. In these situations place your fingers silently over the black keys and your thumb will play on the first white key that occurs. Curl your thumb under your hand before you begin and it will be ready and waiting when it needs to play.

You will often be playing long phrases and it is usual to use your second, third and/or fourth fingers on the black keys because, being longer, they can reach them more easily. Only when you come to octave black key chords do you move your whole hand well forward so that thumb and fifth finger are comfortably over those keys.

In printed music, editors often suggest the best fingering to use. Try it. It may suit your hand and save you time in working it out for yourself. However, everyone's hands are unique so if yours find the editor's ideas unwieldy work out your own fingering, write it on the music – and *stick* to it! Fingers have a muscle memory and if you keep changing their order you may never be able to play the piece well.

When you come to a really difficult phrase, treat it as a challenge. Lift it out of context and practise it on its own, using the best fingering for your hands, until it is as easy as the rest of the piece. Then return it to its rightful position.

21

Compound time

You already know that when you see a triplet ♪♪♪ (3) it means that the three notes are to be played in the time of two of the same value.

So far you have been playing pieces in simple time, where the beats can be halved, quartered etc. and may contain an occasional triplet to give interest to the rhythm.

However, when most or all beats are triplet beats – such as in an Irish jig – having to draw a curved line and italic 3 over every group of three notes, all through the piece, was far too time consuming and tedious for our composers, whose only interest was in getting their latest masterpiece down on paper before they forgot it:

Being inventive types, they came up with yet another shortcut and called it compound time.

Music in compound time has a delicious lilt to it, causing toes to tap and heads to rock:

Note that whole beat notes are 'dotted' to represent the third 'syllable'.

piano

Figure 21.1 shows the compound time signatures, where each beat is divisible by three (i.e. 'beau-ti-ful o-ran-ges').

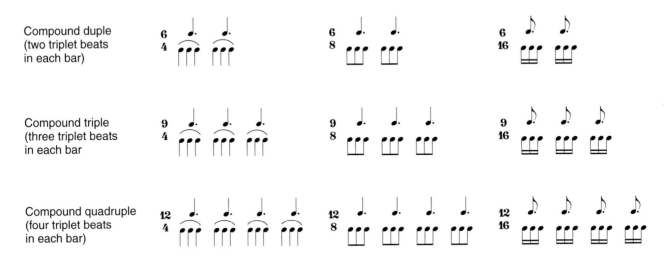

Compound duple (two triplet beats in each bar)

Compound triple (three triplet beats in each bar

Compound quadruple (four triplet beats in each bar)

■ Figure 21.1

The easiest way to work out how many beats there are in each bar of compound time is to divide the top number by three:

Compound duple = 3 into (top number) 6 = two dotted beats in each bar

Compound triple = 3 into 9 = three dotted beats in each bar

Compound quadruple = 3 into 12 = four dotted beats in each bar

Note that the *top* numbers in compound time are 6, 9 and 12 while in simple time they are 2, 3 and 4 (very occasionally 5 or 7 when the composer could be writing for, say, a horse with five legs or an octopus with one tentacle missing).

Like simple time signatures, compound time signatures appear once, immediately after the clefs and Key signature unless the composer wants to change it in a different section of the piece in which case the new time signature will appear.

22

Pedal without blurs

M ost pianos have two pedals, a soft pedal and a sustaining pedal. If yours has a third, central, pedal you can probably ignore it – it will most likely be a 'practice pedal' that will dumb and numb your playing until even you, let alone the neighbours, are unable to hear the music. Not very helpful when you want to bring colour and life to your pieces!

Some grand pianos have a third pedal that when depressed, sustains only the note or chord that is played simultaneously – and nothing subsequently. Very useful when playing music by Debussy but quite unnecessary for any but advanced pianists.

The left pedal is called the soft pedal. If you have an upright piano look down through the lid while your left foot presses that pedal down – release – down – release. You should see all the hammers swinging forward when the pedal is pressed, giving them less far to go to strike the strings. Think of chopping wood. The nearer the axe to the block of wood the smaller will be your swing and the weaker will be your strike.

In a grand piano the soft pedal slides the entire keyboard a couple of centimetres to the right so that only one string can be struck.

When you are required to use the soft pedal the letters *UC* (standing for **una corda** – 'one string' of the pair of thick bass strings) will be printed on the music above or below the notes to be hushed. You may not notice a lot of difference to the sound unless you play very softly while you hold the pedal down. You must release it again when you see the letters *TC* (**tre corde** = three strings).

This pedal is not very often used and requires no special technique.

The right pedal is the sustaining pedal and needs great care and awareness. Open the top piano lid again, look inside and press the sustaining pedal with your right foot.

This time you will see that all the dampers are held away from the strings for as long as the pedal is depressed. With every string free to vibrate, try shouting into the piano. You will hear a mush of sounds that ceases immediately you release that pedal and allow the dampers to return to rest on the strings.

This sustaining pedal is used a great deal – sometimes overused by amateurs in their attempt to conceal wrong notes or the roughness of their technique. At such times it merely results in a horribly blurred and discordant *noise*! This pedal is sometimes wrongly called the 'loud' pedal but if properly used it enriches the sounds for, besides the strings whose keys you are playing, the other strings – whose dampers are also off – will vibrate gently in sympathy, even though they have not been struck by their hammers.

Controlled use of this sustaining pedal produces the most beautiful **cantabile** playing and is especially useful when you want to join the sound of one note or chord to another outside your hand stretch so that they sing on together without a break.

The trick to good pedalling is learning to lose one harmony *as* you play the next (perhaps clashing) one, without causing a gap or a blur.

Musicians say: 'PEDAL WITH YOUR EARS.'

However beautiful a piece and however well it is played, random pedalling can reduce it to a blurred mess. Really good pedalling, however, can lift even a simple piece into a fine performance.

Fine pedalling is simply a matter of good timing – much as changing gear in the car can either cause it to purr smoothly through the changes or 'bunny hop' all down the road.

Here is a short exercise that will enable you to concentrate solely on the pedalling (see Figure 22.1).

Always keeping your right heel on the floor (for stability and control), play the five fingers of your right hand from C to D while depressing and raising your pedal as you change notes. DON'T FORGET TO LISTEN!

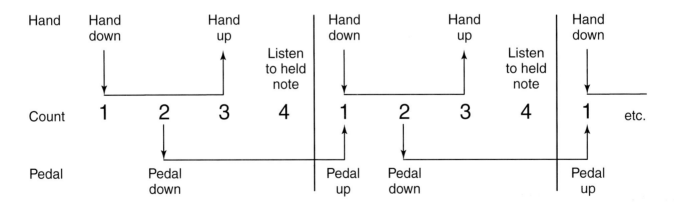

Figure 22.1

When you can play those five notes without any gaps or blurs and are finding the coordination quite easy, try this short piece (Figure 22.2), 'changing' the pedal (raising up and down again) every time you see a ↓_____↑ . Remember, release it *as* you change the harmony and depress it again immediately after the note has sounded.

Figure 22.2

Some printed pedalling marks are worse than vague. If you stick to the technique given here, *never* pedalling during runs (where it would cause blurs), there will be no complaints!

Feel free to experiment by adding either kind of pedalling to any of your pieces that you think would be enhanced.

23

Playing jumps

When one hand has to make a succession of alternating leaps up and down the keyboard it can be quite difficult to strike the right note every time, as we can see in Figure 23.1.

■ Figure 23.1

There is a clever trick for learning this sort of music.

1 Take the bass first. Learn the top line of chords and notes first. This has a melody of its own.

2 Imagine the lower bass line is another melody and learn it the same way.

3 When both are safe play the first note of the lower bass tune while *looking up* at the first chord of the higher bass tune – then jump your hand to it. Your hand will follow your eyes, springing up to the chord.

4 As you play the chord immediately look down to the next low key – and at the right moment let your hand leave its high position and follow your eye downwards.

And so on, looking ahead of the key you are playing as if your hand is always one jump behind your eyes.

Don't take on more than four springs in any practice. It is much more important to get this amount right than to battle through the whole phrase, ending in a worse muddle than you began.

As soon as possible, memorize the 'jumping' phrase for that hand alone so that you won't be continually glancing up and down from music to keys – doubtless with hesitations as you try to find your place. As soon as you are confident you can add the sustaining pedal to bring extra richness to the music.

You have almost certainly heard of Frederic Chopin, one of the great romantic composers. Of French origin, he lived in Warsaw from a few months of age until he left the conservatoire. In much of Chopin's piano music the LH leaps from low notes to expressive chords in the bass clef while heartbreaking RH melodies swirl and soar over the treble keys.

It is said that: 'A poet lives in an ordinary world but has one less layer of skin than other people.' I suggest that Frederick Chopin had two fewer layers than the rest of us, overreacting to life's every situation.

Chopin was born in 1810 to musical parents. His mother played the piano and his father too – when he could get time off from his demanding appointment of professor of French at the university.

Chopin was a gifted and highly sensitive child. At the age of four he only had to hear his older sister practising a new piece and he would sit down straight away and play it perfectly – and beautifully. At six he started piano lessons and after only a year he was being invited to play at musical soirées in his home town – and later, but while still a child, to audiences in packed concert halls.

After leaving Warsaw Conservatoire he toured Europe, giving recitals of his own compositions. It was while he was visiting Stuttgart that he learned of the fall of his beloved Warsaw to the Russians. He was distraught. His Etude Opus 10, no. 12, the 'Revolutionary', is said to have been composed at that time. No doubt he was full of despair and impotent plans for revenge, much as anyone would be.

But Frederic Chopin was not 'anyone'. His emotions were raw and his grief terrible.

Borrow, or better, buy a CD of his Etudes, Opus 10. Their moods range from serene to furious to desperate. All are absolutely beautiful. Borrow the music book from the library and follow them as they are played.

Chopin's music is much too difficult for elementary pianists and you are unlikely to be able to tackle anything he wrote within four or five years, after which you will probably start with his mazurkas (Polish folk dances) or waltzes.

However, a French composer, Erik Satie, wrote 'Three Gymnopedies for the Piano' that are composed along similar lines to many of Chopin's works in that they, too, have a 'leaping bass'. However, while they are very beautiful, they are also quite slow and neither long nor too difficult. They are, in fact, most rewarding to play and ideal for practising singing *legato* melodies over LH leaps – with pedal!

Buy a copy, learn one – and revel in the discovery that you are now a real pianist and musician!

24

Ornaments – taming the twiddles

Quite competent pianists often panic when they come across even the simplest ornament. Their eyes widen fearfully, their body stiffens and they may even hold their breath. Their suddenly tense movements produce jerky, bumpy sounds unfitted to the often delicate music.

Ornaments are simply decorations comprising little twirls of notes to add colour and interest to music that might otherwise be overplain.

To avoid repeatedly writing out these note patterns, composers devised signs to put over, under or between the notes to be decorated. Composers' shorthand again!

These innocent little signs are what so many pianists find terrifying but there is really no need to be frightened of them. Ornaments are not difficult to play. Your very first finger exercise, the one you practised on the table even before your piano arrived, is the basis of all ornament playing – and after a few days you had no trouble with that!

How did ornaments come about?

Before the piano was developed the earliest keyboard instruments, spinets and virginals, produced soft 'plinking' sounds ideal for young ladies to play at polite musical soirées. Goose quills plucked the short strings and it was impossible for the performer to play *legato cantabile* (smoothly and singing) for there were no dampers or pedals as today. Had it not been for the ingenuity of the composer and performer, the sounds would always have died immediately.

To avoid leaving a melody without a sustained supporting harmony or to ensure that a melody note continued to sing on, composers wrote signs indicating that 'trills' – two adjacent notes alternating as rapidly as the player could manage – should be played.

The harpsichord, also a plucked string instrument, was much larger than the spinet or virginal and often combined with an orchestra. It had quite a loud, brash sound and, like the other plucked string instruments, many people found it quite monotonous to listen to when played as a solo.

Adding ornaments to some notes – especially melody notes – gave even a harpsichord piece a certain sparkle and 'trilling' a bass note with its nextdoor neighbour prevented a thin harmony from fading away and leaving an essentially *staccato* melody without any support.

Composers, desperate to get the sounds they wanted from instruments that couldn't produce them, devised several types of ornament to 'help out'. Even when the next stage in the evolution of the piano, the clavichord, came along – in which the goose quills were replaced by little metal hammers that struck the strings – ornaments continued to be invaluable and effective.

The design of the clavichord was still pretty basic and remained so until 1709 when Bartolommeo Cristofori developed the first piano from its fragile antecedents by working out how to get a much wider and more pleasant dynamic range.

Cristofori swapped the clavichord's clangy metal hammers for wooden ones and covered them with soft leather. Then he added dampers – and the piano was born! He called his new instrument a 'gravicembalo col piano e forte' ('a keyboard instrument with soft and loud').

Naturally, it was not as refined as our modern instruments. Among other things, the hammers and dampers are now covered with felt – so much softer than leather – and pedals have been added.

But Cristofori's modifications meant that, for the first time, musicians had a keyboard instrument on which they could play both long and short, soft and loud sounds simultaneously – and even one hand loud, the other soft – and with many degrees of dynamics in between.

The correct name for today's instrument is still the 'Pianoforte'.

You are playing on a soft/loud whose design is basically the same as that of Cristofori's.

Even with their new toy, the 'soft/loud', composers still liked to decorate their music and invented different signs to suit each ornament. These are the ones most usually met with.

The grace note or **acciacatura** , a tiny note written against the main note to be played as if by mistake, squashed against the main note

The **appogiatura** , two or more small melody notes leading lightly onto the main note

The **trill** or **shake** – two adjacent notes rapidly alternating for the duration of the following wavy line

tr 〰〰〰〰〰 = ♩♩♩ ♩♩♩ ♩♩♩ etc.

The **mordent** ♩ = ♩♩♩ and appears ♩♩♩.

The **lower mordent** ♩ = ♩♩♩ and appears ♩♩♩.

A **turn** ∞ is played =

An **inverted turn** is played =

piano

Ornaments can be played upwards or downwards, whichever leads the music smoothly and neatly into the next note or phrase.

One of the greatest composers of those times, Johann Sebastian Bach was born in 1685, 30 years after Cristofori, but well before the latter had developed his 'soft/loud'. Bach therefore had to put up with the harpsichord and what must have been the tinny-sounding clavichord. But with generations of musical ancestors before him, he knew what he wanted.

Despite its limitations he composed widely for the clavichord and harpsichord. His 48 preludes and fugues – *Das Wohltemperierte Klavier* – and the delightful French and English suites (sets of dances of the time) are still played and loved today. He also composed many pieces for his students sprinkling them with ornaments to convey his ideas. He wrote a special book of pieces for his second wife, Anna Magdalena, and that, again, is popular among today's students.

Bach had other ways to achieve the sounds he wanted. During his career he spent time as organist and choirmaster in St Thomas's Church, Leipzig. There he composed passions, cantatas and oratorios for his choirs, thus producing the wide dynamic and emotional ranges that he craved and that were lacking in the keyboard instruments in his home. Nevertheless, the clavichords were in constant use by his students and his own 21 children.

His outsized family and full-time jobs should have been enough for anyone. But in the dining hall of his own home he also tutored the choir boys in harmony and counterpoint, along with keyboard lessons for his children and students. A cheerful fellow, his energy was boundless. What a man!

To practise any ornament poise your hand a little higher than usual over the keyboard, with your fingers resting lightly on the key surfaces.

For a *tr* 〰 play any two adjacent keys alternately and evenly. Later you will be able to play them quickly but keep your trill at a comfortable speed for now.

For mordents 〰 or 〰 'tickle' two adjacent keys 'there and back'. When this is easy descend through any five notes with right hand fingers: 5, 4, 3, 232, 1:

thus producing an upper mordent in a simple scale passage.

Reverse the figure for a lower mordent by playing up the five notes, 1, 2, 3, 434, 5:

Practise these with any pairs of fingers.

When you have a sequence of several mordents it helps to adjust your fingering to avoid breaks in the *legato*.

The left hand is usually harder to control (unless you are left handed, of course!) but a few minutes extra practice will help.

A useful trick when practising an ornament or a long 'run' of notes is to play its last note, then move forward to complete the phrase. Then start two notes from the end of the ornament. Work backwards, bringing in the notes one by one, each time playing on to the end of the phrase.

If the same light touch is used for all the ornaments, you will soon be delighted with the result.

The ever-awkward fourth fingers will probably remain sulkily clumsy. Extra practice may help but as a last resort you might prefer to rearrange your fingering to avoid using it during an ornament.

Always use secure fingering. Try out the given order first (it may save you a lot of time in trying to work out your own) but remember that the editor's ideas may not suit your very individual hand. If so, find a sequence of fingering that does – and stick to it! However perfectly you perform an ornament, you will be let down if it is followed by untimely 'hiccups' as you juggle your fingers to get to the end of the phrase.

Composers of different generations and styles intended different interpretations from similar squiggly handwritten signs and if Beethoven were desperate to capture one idea before he forgot the next he probably wouldn't have drawn very precise 'twiddles' above the notes he wanted to decorate.

By the time the revising horde of scholars and editors have had a go too ('Haydn couldn't have meant that – let's have one of these instead' or 'Students can't manage this ornament at grade 4, let's simplify it') who knows what the composers really intended?

But the meaning of most ornaments is pretty clear so we must do our best to carry it out.

Composer/pianists, such as Frederick Chopin and Franz Liszt loved showing off their brilliant technique and would add flourishing handfuls of glittering notes to amaze their audience.

Watching the virtuoso's performance the audience would be worked up into breathless admiration – tinged with anticipation of the almost unheard of – but still just possible – stumble, just as the crowd watching an international horse show await the 'oooh!' moment when a brilliant rider flies over the fence minus his horse.

Alas, we are not all gifted with naturally 'runny fingers' and may never quite get that sparkle into our playing. We may even have to cut out a few notes to keep the pulse steady as we try to cram 17 tiny notes into one beat, but with real practice (rather than just sitting at the piano and ambling through familiar pieces) the improvement in our technique can be amazing.

25

Syncopation

When you can hold a steady pulse you can begin to think about disturbing the usual strong–weak stresses.

As you already know, the first beat in a bar is normally the strongest.

Sometimes, however, especially in jazz, blues and rhythm music, this stressed beat is delayed beyond where we expect it to be. A normally weak beat, or even part of beat, is accented – giving us the feeling of 'missing the edge of the pavement and arriving too soon on the road'. Placing a rest for the main beat or an accent on one of the following weak notes often shows this.

When learning this kind of music it is a good plan to make sure of the notes initially without upsetting the normal pulse. Once the notes are learned and the beat is overall steady you can start to 'throw' the rhythm to great effect. You will find pieces using syncopation in the jazz books listed in the 'Books you will enjoy' section at the end of the book.

26

Overcoming stage fright

You do not need to be a concert pianist to suffer from stage fright. Even if you are only playing to your neighbour you can be assaulted by nerves and make silly mistakes.

Should you feel confident enough to show off your new talent to a crowd of friends you can find that your hands are suddenly sweaty, your heart rate has doubled and you wish yourself anywhere but sitting at your piano.

Nerves are not an affliction, the trick lies in learning to control and use them to give that extra life and sparkle to your performance. Without nerves you would probably play like a robot! Even so, few of us play our best in front of an audience, certainly in our early learning years. That is perfectly normal but no reason to hide yourself and your music away. Far better to face the problems and take steps to overcome them.

You need to know your piece really well – if possible, to be able to play it by heart. Then, consciously, recheck the bass, then the treble, then both hands together. Having done that there are three more stages of learning for performance:

1 Be able to pick up the music anywhere in the piece.

2 Play beautifully and easily to yourself.

3 Play equally well to one friend.

If your playing is really secure you are more likely to give your best performance.

Playing a loved piece so often that it becomes stale causes a problem. You lose concentration and switch over to 'automatic pilot'. Your mischievous fingers suddenly find themselves free from 'brain control' and you are only saved by your faithful, ever-alert ears picking up the errors and reawakening your brain. All you can do is play the piece through once more, very slowly and perhaps with each hand separately before putting it away and starting on something else. A few days later bring it out again and it will once more be fresh and beautiful.

Be aware that your movements may become slightly restricted when you are under any sort of stress. Your LH might not quite reach that low note or your RH may fumble a chord. Such annoying mishaps are possible so if a stumble should occur, be a 'hit and run driver' and (as we saw in Unit 16) KEEP GOING, if necessary picking up the music at the next phrase.

Everyone slips up sometimes so, when you do, don't let it throw you. Just smile – and carry on.

Never let anyone talk you into playing 'off the cuff'. That said, it is always wise to have a few pieces that you love 'up your sleeve' in case the atmosphere is congenial and the idea of playing appeals to you – perhaps to give pleasure to an elderly friend.

Until you feel really confident, don't 'show off' by playing a piece that taxes your budding technique. There lurks disaster! Far better to play something simple and really familiar so that you, too, can relax and enjoy the experience.

Remember: 'It ain't *what* you play – it's the way that you play it.'

When you are ready take a deep breath, concentrate, 'lift on', smile – and off you go. Ignore the jet that passes overhead just as you reach the quiet phrase, block out someone's mobile phone that joins in with its own jangle and endure the cat that saunters over to sit on your feet when you are about to use the pedals. If you appear relaxed and happy, both you and your audience will enjoy the music.

A true example of professionalism occurred when a famous quartet was playing in a French concert hall on a hot and humid July evening. The stage lights were on; all the windows open. Alas, no sooner did the players begin than, seemingly, every insect for miles around flew in to buzz angrily around the musicians. Not content with biting the deliciously warm necks and hands, some minute black bugs decided to wander all over the music, making it appear a totally different and ever-changing piece from that which the composer had intended and the musicians had rehearsed.

As for the poor unfortunate pianist, many creatures were also attracted to the keys so that he was constantly having to decide, 'To squash or not to squash?' as he played.

Somehow the performers carried on as if nothing was amiss and only the front three rows had witnessed what, but for the players' fine preparation, could have been a total musical disaster!

27

Where do you go from here?

If you have enjoyed working through this book and your piano time has become an essential part of every day, CONGRATULATIONS! Hopefully, you will want to move on, far beyond your present level of achievement. If this is so your best bet is to find a good teacher to guide you and introduce you to some of the wealth of music of the kind you most enjoy. Your new skills will be equally valuable for whatever style you want to play from classical to romantic, jazz to ragtime, rhythm to blues, music from the shows.

How can you find the right teacher for *you*? You may have friends who are learning your type of music or your nearest music shop will probably have a list of local teachers. The manager should be able to advise you of those most suited to your requirements. Some teachers take only children; some only do exam work; others accept only beginners but there will be many fine teachers able and willing to help you in whatever way you want to develop.

Many quite small towns hold competitive music festivals with classes in most styles. These usually take place during spring or summer but there is no rule about this. Get the (usually free) syllabuses from your music shop or library and attend some of the festival classes. Entry fees for non-players for each session – morning, afternoon or evening – usually only cover the cost of a programme.

You can learn much about the teachers' work by hearing their pupils' performance.

While many teenage – and some adult – competitors find playing to an audience of strangers very nerve wracking, and their playing obviously not up to their usual standard, you may get a better idea of which teacher would suit you by going along to the under-15 classes.

It is comparatively easy to spot the teachers in the audience – they usually have a knot of candidates and parents round them!

This is your time to observe! Do the teachers smile and chat with the parents? Do the competitors look relaxed and cheerful? When it is their turn to play do they sit comfortably and correctly at the piano? Do they then play musically – or thump like blocks of wood? Are they praised after their performance and reassured if their playing came to grief? Youngsters often lack concentration and can make a horrible mess of their pieces just when they want to play them beautifully.

If you have decided to continue to expand your music any happy teacher (and there are plenty about) might suit you very well.

Find out names – the door attendants usually know them all or ask a member of the festival committee who are always in attendance – then ring and make an appointment.

Don't be put off if the first one you try has a full list. That is a good sign and you can either ring another teacher or carry on as you are while waiting until a vacancy occurs with your first choice.

If you decide to wait you can keep up your skills and discover new ideas with the pieces that you haven't yet learned among the suggested books. You might borrow some from the library or again visit your friendly music shop manager and let him show you a selection. He may even be able to play some through for you to choose from.

Whatever you decide, GOOD LUCK! Go on playing, moving forward and loving your music!

Books you will enjoy

There are literally thousands of music books on the market but, in order of difficulty, here are some you could try after you have played 'The Pessimist'.

For the first year aim to start a new short piece and polish your last one every week.
Move on to another book whenever you feel ready.

Folk Songs (arr. Carol Barratt)   Chester Music.

Graded Pieces for Piano – Bk One (preliminary) (James Ching)   EMI Music.

Making the Grade – Bk One (popular) (Lynda Frith)   Chester Music.

A Feast of Carols (arr. Carol Barratt)   Chester Music.

Alfred's Piano Library Repertoire – Level 2 (Classics)   Alfred Publishing.

A Little Notebook for Anna Magdalena Bach (J.S. Bach)   Alfred Publishing.

Three Gymnopedies – for leaping and pedalling (Eric Satie)   Alfred Publishing.

Any book of easiest pieces that attracts you for exploring without learning.

And for anyone inclined towards jazz, blues etc, again in order of difficulty:

Microjazz for Beginners – Level 2 (tips on playing jazz) (Christopher Norton)   Boosey & Hawkes.

Piano Time Jazz (Pauline Hall)   Oxford University Press.

Jazz, Rags and Blues – Bk One (Martha Mier)   Alfred Publishing.

Melodies with Max (Myrna Stent)   Kevin Meyhew.

Any book of songs from the shows (easy piano arrangement)   Various.

The Joy of George Gershwin, Yorktown Music Press.

Many of these books are in series, so if you like them you can move on to the next one up when you feel ready.

Musical terms you may meet

Terms of speed

adagio = very slow

largo = slow and stately

lento = slow

andante = walking pace

comodo = at an easy pace

allegretto = fast walking pace

allegro = fast and lively

presto = very fast

prestissimo = as fast as possible

Terms of change of speed

accelerando (accel.) = gradually getting faster

allargando = broadening out; gradually slowing down

calando = decreasing both in tone and speed

meno mosso = with less movement (slower)

rallentando (rall.) = gradually slowing down

ritenuto (rit.) = slower at once

rubato = 'robbed' time, soon to be made up

stringendo = with increasing speed

Terms of dynamics

forte (*f*) = loud

fortissimo (*ff*) = very loud

mezzo forte (*mf*) = half (moderately) loud

mezzo piano (*mp*) = half (moderately) soft

pianissimo (*pp*) = very soft

piano (*p*) = soft

Terms to show change of dynamics

calando = gradually softer and slower

crescendo (cresc) = gradually getting louder

decrescendo (decresc) = gradually getting softer

diminuendo (dim) = getting softer

morendo = dying away

perdendosi = decreasing both in tone and speed ('losing itself')

sforzando = with sudden force

smorzando = dying away

Some terms to show how a piece is to be played

agitato = agitated

appassionato = with passion

cantabile = in a singing style

delicato = delicately

dolente = sadly

*espressione = expression

fine = the end

furioso = furiously

giusto = in strict time

animato = animated

brilliante = with sparkle

deciso = decisively

dolce = sweetly

*energico = with energy

espressivo = with expression

*fuoco = fire

giocoso = joyously

grazioso = gracefully

legato = smoothly

lunga pausa = a long pause

mesto = sadly

pastorale = in a pastoral, country style

risoluto = resolutely

scherzando = playfully

staccato = detached

subito = suddenly, at once

tranquillo = peacefully

vivo = lively

leggiero = lightly

lusingando = coaxing

parlando = in a speaking style

pesante = heavily

ritmico = rhythmically

sostenuto = sustained

strepitoso = noisy, boisterous

teneramente = tenderly

vivace = quick, lively

volente = flying

* *con* (*with*) usually appears with these

Miscellaneous

attacca = go on at once

ben = well (e.g. *ben marcato* = well marked)

cadence = the end of a phrase (esp. the last two chords)

coda = a final section to round a piece off neatly

con = with (e.g. *con spirito* = with spirit)

corda = a string

glissando (gliss) = rapid slide of notes up or down the keyboard

ma non troppo = but not too much (e.g. *allegro ma non troppo*)

main droite = MD (French) = play with the right hand

main gauche = MG (French) = play with the left hand

mano destra = MD (Italian) = play with the right hand

mano sinistra = MS (Italian) = play with the left hand

meno = less (*meno mosso* = less movement – a little slower)

ossia = otherwise (a second way of playing the phrase)

piu = more (*piu mosso* = more movement – a little faster) *poco a poco* = little by little

primo = first

quasi = almost

rinforzando = with extra emphasis

scherzo = a joke

segno = a sign (*dal segno* = repeat from the sign)

senza = without (e.g. *senza rallentando* = without slowing down)

simile = in the same way

stanza = a verse of a song

tempo = the speed

tempo giusto = strict time

tempo primo = return to original speed (after varying it)

tenuto (*ten.*) = held, sustained

troppo = too much (*allegro non troppo* = fast but not too fast)

volti subito = turn over quickly

Glossary

accent = when a *key* is struck sharply to make the sound stand out

acciaccatura = an *ornament*

appogiatura = an *ornament*

aria = a song

bagatelle = a short piece

ballade = a simple composition with a strong melody

barcarolle = a boat song – a piece with a gentle rocking movement

beat = the regular *pulse* of the music

berceuse = a cradle song, a quiet piece with a rocking *pulse*

bolero = a lively Spanish dance in a set rhythm

cadenza = a brilliant passage during a *concerto* for the soloist to show off

canon = imitation of the theme in other parts or voices so that they continue together

capriccio = a caprice; a light, free piece with no special form

cavatina = a short piece, usually for voices

clef = a sign drawn on the *stave* to show where the music is to be played

coda = a 'tail piece' to conclude a piece

compound time = when each *beat* is dotted, therefore divisible by three

concerto = a major composition for orchestra and soloist, usually in *sonata* form with three or four *movements*

counterpoint (lit 'note against note') = two or more different melodies singing together

dampers = felt-covered wooden blocks preventing the strings from vibrating unless their *key* is played

etude = a study – a work to develop a student's technique

form = the structure of a musical composition

fugue = a contrapuntal (*counterpoint*) piece usually written for three or more 'voices' (but often played by one person whose control is such that each melody can be heard in turn)

gavotte = a dignified French dance usually part of a *suite*

gigue = a fast, lively dance, usually part of a *suite*

hammers = felt-covered wooden hammers that strike the strings when the keys are played

harmony = a blend of sounds making a concord or a discord

impromptu = an improvised piece

interval = the distance in pitch between notes

invention = a short contrapuntal piece

key = the black and white keys on a keyboard that are depressed by the pianist; *also* the scale whose notes have been used for the composition

Key signature = sharps or flats placed immediately after the clefs to show which *Key* the piece is in

mazurka = a Polish dance in triple time (unusually, the second *beat* of each bar is accented)

minuet = a stately dance in triple time, often found in a *suite*

modulation = the act of moving a piece from one *Key* to another, usually to change its mood

mordent = an *ornament*

movement = one of (usually) three or more sections of a major musical work

musette = a short, pastoral piece sometimes following a *gavotte*

nocturne = a night piece, usually lyrical and dreamy

opus = a set of compositions published together. Opus 3 = the third set of the composer's works

oratorio = orchestral setting for a biblical story with chorus and soloists

ornament = musical decoration

overture = orchestral introduction to an opera

partita = another name for a *suite*

phrase = a musical sentence

prelude = a short piece, often an introduction

pulse = the regular throb, or *beat*, of the music

rondo = a 'sandwich' piece when the main theme recurs several times

simple time = each beat can be halved, quartered, i.e. divisible by two

slur = a small group of two or more notes to be played *legato*, the last one to be lifted off lightly

sonata = a work for one or more instruments with (usually) three or four *movements*, originally in a set form, now often with two or more movements running freely without breaks

sonatina = a shorter and simpler form of *sonata*, usually with only two *movements*

stave (staff) = groups of five lines that, with the *clef*, position the notes on the keyboard

suite = a set of classical dances (e.g. allemande, minuet, gigue etc.)

symphony = a work in *sonata* form for orchestra.

tarantella = a lively dance once played when a boy was bitten by a poisonous spider and he danced until he sweated the venom out . . . or he died!

tempo = the overall speed of the music

tie = a curved line over two or more notes or chords, prolonging their sound as far as required without playing them again

time signature = two numbers at the start of a piece showing the number and value of beats in each bar

transposing = moving the music into another key – perhaps for a singer whose voice cannot reach the pitch of the key in which the piece has been written

trill or **shake** = an *ornament*

triplet = three notes to be played in the time of two of the same value

una corda = 'one string' = use the soft pedal (**tre corda** = release the soft pedal)

volti subito (*VS*) = turn the page quickly

Index